"Pat Williams has captured the essence of every successful person: it's never complicated. Their secrets are always simple and succinct. This isn't just a book, it's a companion to be read and reread many times."

—**Ernie Accorsi**, longtime NFL executive

"Pat Williams has been an important part of the sports world for a long time, and along the way he has met a lot of interesting personalities including Sandy Koufax, Pete Maravich, and Kevin Durant. But as you will see in this fine book, Pat Williams is more interesting than any of them. His stories about the rich and famous will inspire you and make you smile. Consider yourself lucky to have spent quality time with the always entertaining Mr. Williams."

—**Peter Golenbock**, bestselling sports author

"Pat Williams's new book is packed with fascinating stories and life lessons for all ages. This may be his best book yet."

—**Jerry Reinsdorf**, Chicago White Sox chairman

"I love Pat Williams, but I don't understand him. How can someone be so relentlessly optimistic? Every book he writes leaves you feeling better than when you started, and *It's Not Who You Know, It's Who You Are* is the latest example. He may also have met every single famous person alive, and you will hear from them, or about them, in this delightful tome."

—**Bob Ryan**, *Boston Globe*/ESPN

"Pat Williams has always served as an inspiration to many, and now he's compiled some of the best stories I've ever read which will inspire you if you're an athlete, a business person, or a parent. These stories are absolute gems which you'll want to read and read again and again and again. *It's Not Who You Know, It's Who You Are* is a winner—just like Pat."

—**Ernie Johnson**, *Inside the NBA on TNT* studio host

"No one has studied leadership, success, and winning more than Pat Williams. There is hardly a winner in the sports world (or any other part of society) that Pat has not studied and talked to. The lessons from *It's Not Who You Know, It's Who You Are* will impact anyone in any profession."

—**Stan Van Gundy**, Detroit Pistons president of basketball operations and head coach

"Pat Williams has amassed a collection of fascinating stories and anecdotes over his long career in sports. I had a hard time putting this book down; you will too."

—**Marv Albert**, Basketball Hall of Fame sportscaster

"In today's sound-bite world, Pat has captured the characteristics of successful leaders in sports, politics, and business through quick and powerful stories. Each vignette provides insight for success and the traits that led to outstanding careers by people who we always recognized as leaders—and now we know why they were so successful. Pat has hit another 'grand slam' with this book!"

—**Ron Wellman**, Wake Forest University director of athletics

"*It's Not Who You Know, It's Who You Are* is a must-read not only for sports fans but for anyone who wants to achieve success in life. Pat Williams has enjoyed a remarkable career and shares with the reader the life lessons that he's learned from a wide variety of people. It's truly an inspiring book."

—**Mark Murphy**, Green Bay Packers president and chief executive officer

"Thank you, Pat, for sharing the life lessons you've learned from these inspiring winners. Dad would have been honored that you included him in your latest book. You're a winner in my eyes!"

—**Nan Wooden**, daughter of Coach John Wooden

"Pat Williams has done it again! His new book is loaded with great material, amusing anecdotes, and inspiring stories. This is a wonderful book that I could not put down."

—**Wayne Embry**, Basketball Hall of Famer

"*It's Not Who You Know, It's Who You Are* is filled with a lot of success stories and nuggets of inspiration that can help us at any level that we're at. I love how Pat is able to share so many stories that lighten the mood and set the stage for us becoming better people. Truly a great read showcasing lots of great people. There's something for everyone."

—**Tamika Catchings**, WNBA All Star

"I couldn't put this book down. It is loaded with terrific stories, all with a strong message. It's another slam dunk for Pat Williams."

—**Kevin Ollie**, University of Connecticut men's basketball team head coach, 2014 NCAA champion

"Pat Williams is a great storyteller. This latest collection is filled with good life lessons. I had a hard time putting the book down."

—**Steve Clifford**, Charlotte Hornets head coach

IT'S NOT WHO YOU KNOW, IT'S WHO YOU ARE

IT'S NOT WHO YOU KNOW, IT'S WHO YOU ARE

Life Lessons from Winners

PAT WILLIAMS
with **JIM DENNEY**

Revell

a division of Baker Publishing Group
Grand Rapids, Michigan

Published by Revell
a division of Baker Publishing Group
P.O. Box 6287, Grand Rapids, MI 49516-6287
www.revellbooks.com

Printed in the United States of America

Library of Congress Cataloging-in-Publication Data
Williams, Pat, 1940–
    It's not who you know, it's who you are : life lessons from winners / Pat Williams with Jim Denney.
        pages cm
    Includes bibliographical references.
    ISBN 978-0-8007-2277-7 (cloth)
    1. Celebrities—Conduct of life. 2. Character. 3. Success. 4. Influence (Psychology)—Religious aspects—Christianity. I. Denney, Jim, 1953– II. Title.
BJ1521.W59 2015
650.1—dc23   2014029693

15 16 17 18 19 20 21   7 6 5 4 3 2 1

In keeping with biblical principles of creation stewardship, Baker Publishing Group advocates the responsible use of our natural resources. As a member of the Green Press Initiative, our company uses recycled paper when possible. The text paper of this book is composed in part of post-consumer waste.

To the late Bob Carpenter and his son, Ruly, my good friend, in gratitude for the opportunity they gave me as a young ballplayer and front office exec. They made all these stories possible.

Contents

Contents

Contents

Contents

Foreword

As a longtime sports executive and author, Pat Williams has met seemingly everybody. Not only has he met them but he has interacted with them on a meaningful level in one fascinating way or another. In this book, Pat has mined a lifetime of experiences to provide readers with a wide array of anecdotes and stories that are both immensely fun and wonderfully profound.

Pat has long possessed one of the greatest senses of humor in modern sport. For decades, sportswriters have relied on Pat's insight, immense wit, and keen memory to bring their stories alive. *It's Not Who You Know, It's Who You Are* now brings that mother lode of his experiences and memories to his many readers.

Among the multitude of voices, there's the great Bill Veeck, who mentored Pat in the art of sports promotions, and other sports figures such as Ted Williams, Dick Bavetta, Joe Namath and more. It's the kind of volume that's destined to become an instant classic. After all, it just doesn't get any better than Pat Williams on sports and life.

And, as this impressive book clearly demonstrates, he has the memories and experiences to prove it.

Roland Lazenby, legendary sportswriter
and author of *Michael Jordan: The Life*

Acknowledgments

With deep appreciation, I acknowledge the support and guidance of the following people who helped make this book possible.

Special thanks to Alex Martins, Dan DeVos, and Rich DeVos of the Orlando Magic.

Hats off to my associate Andrew Herdliska; my proofreader, Ken Hussar; and my ace typist, Fran Thomas.

Thanks also to my writing partner, Jim Denney, for his superb contributions in shaping this manuscript.

Hearty thanks also go to Andrea Doering, executive editor at Revell Books, and to the entire Revell team for their vision and insight and for believing we had something important to say in these pages.

And, finally, special thanks and appreciation go to my wife, Ruth, and to my wonderful and supportive family. They are truly the backbone of my life.

Introduction

"Keep Your Eyes and Ears Open"

In 1968, I left Minor League Baseball and took my first NBA job. As the business manager of the Philadelphia 76ers, I was in charge of promoting the team and packing people into the arena.

The Phoenix Suns had just entered the league as an expansion team, and their ownership group included a number of famous people, including Henry Mancini and Andy Williams. I read that Andy Williams was performing at a supper club across the river in New Jersey, so I typed up some advertising copy and lugged my portable tape recorder to the club. I managed to fast-talk my way into Andy Williams's dressing room. After the show, he walked into his dressing room—and there I was, waiting for him.

I introduced myself and told him what I wanted him to do. I set up the tape recorder and handed the advertising copy to him. Once the tape was rolling, Andy Williams, in that wonderful "Moon River" voice, recorded a season ticket blurb plus a promo for the Suns-76ers game later in the season.

I had arrived without knowing if I would get within a hundred feet of Andy Williams, and I left with his voice captured on my tape recorder. He had been not only willing to help but also *eager* to help. His endorsement helped sell a lot of tickets and fill a lot of seats that season.

Later that fall, Martha and the Vandellas performed at that same supper club, and I was able to get Martha Reeves to record a voice-over that sounded fantastic with "Heat Wave" playing in the background.

What fun I had! I was all of twenty-eight years old, and I had my first big league job. I believed I could do anything, and I was absolutely fearless when I approached famous people for a favor.

I have nineteen children—four biological kids, fourteen by international adoption, and one by remarriage—and I have encouraged all of them to be bold, to speak up, to introduce themselves, and to ask questions. There have been times when my kids have said to me, "Hey, Dad, I saw Ken Griffey Jr. downtown today," or, "I saw Monica Seles at the mall." I would always say, "That's great! What did you say? What did you ask? What advice did he or she give you?"

And almost always, my kids would reply, "I didn't say anything. I didn't want to intrude."

They didn't want to intrude! Haven't they ever seen ol' Dad in action? Whenever I encounter accomplished people, I speak up. I ask questions. I'm always eager to have some of that person's wisdom, insight, and success rub off on me. If I have time to ask a question or two, I grab my pen and a paper napkin and I fire away: "What's the most important word of advice you ever got? Who were your role models when you were growing up? What can I do to be successful?"

Over the years, I've crossed paths with many famous people, and I've always seized the opportunity. Sure, I've been rebuffed a few times, but so what? I've also accumulated a vast treasure trove of insights—and I've filled this book with those insights.

If you encounter an accomplished, successful person, don't be shy. Don't squander the opportunity. Speak up! Introduce yourself! Ask questions!

I got my first job in professional sports from Bob Carpenter, the owner of the Philadelphia Phillies. He gave me a word of advice before sending me to the Phillies farm club in Miami: "Keep your eyes and ears open—on and off the field."

I've never forgotten that advice. I have always kept my eyes and ears open. I have tried to learn something new every day. I have especially tried to learn life lessons from winners in every walk of life. In these pages, you'll find life lessons I have learned from my encounters with presidents, civil rights leaders, business leaders, sports executives, athletes, religious leaders, entertainers, and more.

I hope you enjoy this book—and maybe find an inspiring insight or two. I also hope you'll write to me and share your thoughts with me. My eyes and ears are wide open, and I'm eager to learn from *you*!

Part 1

★ ★ ★

Success

Stephen Olford

The Dugout Diver

For thirteen years, I coordinated the Philadelphia Phillies chapel services in the clubhouse before the games. Usually the chapel was held in the morning before a one o'clock game, but on one occasion, before a six o'clock Sunday evening game, we had the chapel service at about 4:30. I had arranged for Dr. Stephen Olford to be our speaker. Olford was a preacher from England whom Billy Graham had once called "the man who most influenced my ministry."

After Olford gave the message, he and legendary Phillies third baseman Mike Schmidt talked for a long time. Mike was a new Christian, and he and Olford seemed to hit it off.

At game time, the Phillies arranged for Olford and me to sit in the front row right next to the Phillies' dugout. In the bottom of the first with two men on base, Mike Schmidt came up to bat. The next thing we knew, Mike hammered one far and deep into the left field seats. Fifty thousand Phillies fans went wild as Mike rounded the bases and headed for home.

While I watched all this, Olford leaped out of his seat and started climbing over the railing. For a moment, I was too shocked to move. There was the erudite Olford in his suit and tie and cuff links—and he was making a dive for the dugout! He was so caught up in the excitement that he wanted to go into the dugout and embrace his new best friend, Mike Schmidt!

The stadium security guards ran to Olford and pushed him back toward the stands, and I tried to grab him and pull him from behind. I shouted to him, "Dr. Olford! The fans aren't allowed on the field! And they sure aren't allowed to dive into the dugout!"

He shouted back in his clipped English accent, "I just wanted to congratulate my friend Mike!"

I said, "I'll take you to the locker room after the game. That would probably be more appropriate."

I managed to get Olford back into his seat. But for a few moments, I got to see a reputedly staid and reserved English clergyman go nuts at a Phillies game. No wonder even Billy Graham looked up to this "dugout diver" as a friend and mentor. Stephen Olford was a man who passionately, enthusiastically cheered the success and accomplishments of others.

★ ★ ★

Ted Williams

A Passion to Be the Best

Each year after the Ted Williams Museum and Hitters Hall of Fame induction ceremonies, there is an activity for the attendees, such as a golf or fishing outing.

One year, I elected to go fishing, and one of my companions in the bass boat was the great NBC sportscaster Curt Gowdy. Talk about intimidation! For years, Gowdy hosted *The American Sportsman* and took many sports and entertainment legends out on fishing and hunting expeditions. So I felt both honored and out of my league to be sitting in a boat on a lake in central Florida trying to catch a bass with Curt Gowdy.

I was much more interested in talking to Gowdy than in fishing. Gowdy knew Ted Williams quite well, having been the voice of the Boston Red Sox for fifteen years (in fact, he made the call when Williams hit a home run on his final at bat in 1960). So I asked Gowdy how he would sum up Williams's life and career. He said, "Ted Williams is the only man I've ever met who was the best at what he did in three different fields: the best hitter in baseball, the best at catching fish, and the best Navy combat pilot. Everything Ted Williams does he does with an intense passion to be the best."

★ ★ ★

Jentezen Franklin

"Like a Heat-Seeking Missile"

I once had bestselling author Jentezen Franklin (*Right People, Right Place, Right Plan*) as a guest on my Orlando radio show, and he made a statement that stuck in my mind and that I have quoted often when speaking to audiences: "When you discover your passion in life and pursue it relentlessly, you become like a heat-seeking missile."

There's so much truth packed into that one sentence. Think about it. A heat-seeking missile searches for a source of heat, locks onto it, then chases it with single-minded focus. If the heat source moves up, down, or sideways, the missile follows unerringly. When you are passionate about your goals and dreams, you move unerringly toward the target of your passion. That's why passion is such a powerful ally of success.

It's not enough simply to set some goals, then methodically plod toward them. You've got to get fired up and motivated. Never be content to dwell in the gray margins of life. Become a heat-seeking missile! Live passionately!

★ ★ ★

Ted Williams

The Groove in the Handle

I acquired my obsession with Ted Williams from my mother's younger brother, Bill Parsons. Uncle Bill related everything—and I mean everything!—to the great Red Sox slugger. If I didn't want to eat my brussels sprouts, Uncle Bill would say, "You know, Ted would have eaten his brussels sprouts. You think maybe that's why he's such a great hitter?"

When I was fourteen, my buddy Gil Yule and I would go to Philadelphia to watch the A's play almost every weekend. I saw

Ted Williams in person at an A's–Red Sox doubleheader. My team, the A's, lost both games.

Afterward, Gil and I waited outside the park by the Red Sox bus, and there was Williams walking to the bus as fans called out to him and pulled at him. He climbed into the front seat of the bus with the window open while hordes of kids swarmed around him like mosquitoes in July, begging for his autograph. And I was one of those kids.

Williams stuck his head out the window and roared, "Everybody get in line or I'm not signing!" Well, we all lined up and quieted down, and Williams signed autographs for every kid in line, including young Pat Williams. The picture he signed for me that day is still in my collection.

Gil and I boarded the train to Wilmington, and Dad picked us up at the station. I came bounding into the house, and Mom, who had heard the games on the radio, said, "Oh, son, what a disappointing day! The A's lost twice."

I said, "It was great, Mom! I got Ted Williams's autograph!"

When the Ted Williams Museum and Hitters Hall of Fame opened not far from Orlando, I saw Williams more often. When he entered the room, every conversation stopped and he was the center of attention.

At one induction dinner, a fan went to Williams and held out a bat. "Ted, I've had this bat for a long time," he said. "I'm told that you used it in 1941, the season you hit .406."

Williams took the bat and closed his eyes as he worked his hands around the grip. "Yep," he said, "this is one of my bats. In 1940 and '41, I'd cut a groove in the handle for my right index finger to nestle in. I can feel that groove. This is one of my bats all right."

After sixty years, Williams still recalled the little things that contributed to his greatness.

★ ★ ★

Sam Walton

"Curious about Everything"

After speaking at an event in Fayetteville, Arkansas, I walked to the back of the room and sat down next to a man dressed in khaki slacks and a golf shirt. He leaned toward me and whispered, "Nice job."

"Thank you," I said.

He extended his hand and said, "I'm Jim Walton."

I was amazed. By chance, I had chosen to sit down next to billionaire James Carr Walton, the chairman of Arvest Bank and the youngest son of Sam Walton, the founder of Walmart. According to *Forbes*, he was then the twentieth richest individual on the planet.

"Pleased to meet you, Mr. Walton," I said.

"Call me Jim. Would you like to join me for lunch?"

So we had lunch together. Over turkey on rye sandwiches, I asked him, "Tell me about your dad. What was Sam Walton's greatest strength as a leader?"

"His greatest strength? It would have to be his passion. Dad was passionate about life and passionate about the merchandise. He loved to travel around and see the latest things he could sell in his stores. He was always trying to get the best price on the best merchandise so he could pass the savings on to his customers. Now, take that shirt you're wearing."

Jim pointed to my Hawaiian shirt.

"What about it?" I said.

"Dad would have been fascinated by that shirt. He would

have examined the fabric and asked you where it came from. He would have turned the sleeve inside out and looked at the stitching. He was curious about everything, constantly asking questions and reading up on every aspect of the retail business. That's why he was so good at what he did, and that was his greatest strength as a leader."

★ ✹ ★

Jimmy Valvano

Laugh, Think, and Cry

One of the greatest role models of passionate living I've ever met is the late, great basketball coach Jimmy Valvano, aka "Jimmy V." I knew Valvano when he was coaching the North Carolina State Wolfpack and broadcasting at ABC and ESPN. He was famed for his passionate, optimistic, enthusiastic way of speaking and living. Whenever I spoke to him, I always went away feeling emotionally uplifted.

In June 1992, Valvano was diagnosed with bone cancer—a grim diagnosis—yet he never surrendered his passion for living. On March 4, 1993, Valvano received the Arthur Ashe Courage and Humanitarian Award at the inaugural ESPY Awards event. In his acceptance speech, he talked about living with passion in spite of adversity.

"There are three things we all should do every day," he said. "Number one is laugh. You should laugh every day. Number two is think. You should spend some time in thought. Number three, you should have your emotions move you to tears. It could be happiness or joy. If you laugh, you think, and you cry, that's a full day. That's a heck of a day. You do that seven days a week and you're going to have something special."

Valvano died less than two months after saying those words. He had something special, something we all need. He had an intense, irrepressible passion for living—and that passion lives on after him, setting an example for you and me.

★ ★ ★

Fess Parker

Pay Your Dues

Once in an interview, *Davy Crockett* star Fess Parker recalled how giant radioactive ants helped him land the role of the legendary frontiersman from Tennessee.

"Walt Disney was searching for the right actor to play Davy Crockett," Fess told me. "Just about every Hollywood action guy was considered for the role, including George Montgomery and Ronald Reagan. Somebody told Walt he should look at a sci-fi movie called *Them!* about radioactive giant ants attacking Los Angeles. The star of that film was Jim Arness, who would eventually become Marshal Dillon on *Gunsmoke*.

"Walt screened the picture to scout Jim Arness, but then he spotted me in the film. I had a small speaking part, so small that if you looked away to put cream in your coffee you would have missed me altogether. But Walt said, 'Who's that fella?' Nobody knew. So Tom Blackburn, one of Walt's producers, called Warner Brothers, and they gave him my name. Then Disney called me out to the studio for an interview and a screen test.

"I was twenty-nine at the time, and I fancied myself a singer and songwriter, so I brought my guitar with me. Walt and I talked for a while, and then he said, 'Why don't you play me a little tune?' I had written a song called 'Lonely' about a guy who's riding on a train after breaking up with his girl. I did the sound of a train whistle in the song. I didn't know it then, but Walt Disney had a real passion for railroads, so that little song didn't hurt my chances.

"If I hadn't had that bit part in a movie about giant ants, I might never have had the career I had. Walt spotted me, yanked me out of obscurity, and made me a star. He opened every door for me. I'll always be grateful to Walt Disney."

"So you paid your dues," I said. "You took the bit part, and that's how you got to be 'King of the Wild Frontier.'"

"Something like that."

"Fess, would you indulge me? How about a chorus of 'Davy Crockett'?"

He immediately obliged. I heard that deep, mellow voice sing, "Born on a mountaintop in Tennessee . . ."

I sang along. Fortunately, no tape recorder was running.

★ ★ ★

Sandy Patti

Let Mistakes Refine You, Not Define You

When I was the general manager of the Philadelphia 76ers, we celebrated "God, Family, and Country Night" twice a year. We would bring in gospel singers and athletes to deliver a message of patriotism and faith. One year, we brought in a rising young singer named Sandy Patti to sing the National Anthem, then perform a concert after the game.

I was on the court while Sandy sang the National Anthem, and I noticed that it seemed to go by quickly. When she got to "and the home of the brave," the crowd cheered. Then it was time for the game to begin.

I sat down at courtside and saw Sandy rushing toward me, her hand over her mouth, eyes wide, aghast. She said, "Oh, Mr. Williams, this is terrible! I left out the whole middle stanza!"

Well, that explained why the anthem seemed to go by so quickly.

"Sandy," I said, "you sang so beautifully that no one even noticed."

"But—"

"You did a terrific job. Don't give it another thought."

Not long after that appearance, Sandy Patti shot to stardom. She regularly comes through Orlando to perform concerts, so I have seen her from time to time over the years. Whenever she sees me, she laughs and says, "How about our National Anthem?"

That was more than three decades ago, and she still remembers leaving out the middle stanza. But she's no longer horrified over it. She just laughs.

★ ✸ ★

Billy Cunningham, Jerry Sloan, and Scott Skiles

Be a Ferocious Competitor

Over the many years I've worked in the NBA, I've often been asked if I have a favorite player among all the players I've worked with. You might think my favorite would be a player who's loaded with natural talent like Julius Erving or Shaquille O'Neal or Pete Maravich. But the three players who left the greatest impression on me were Billy Cunningham, who played for the Philadelphia 76ers; Jerry Sloan, who played for the Chicago Bulls; and Scott Skiles, who played for the Orlando Magic.

What did Cunningham, Sloan, and Skiles have in common? They were ferocious competitors. They didn't, in every case, possess the greatest natural talent, but they leveraged the talent they had through a positive attitude, an intense focus, a strong work ethic, and a commitment to teamwork.

Cunningham, Sloan, and Skiles were smart players, but they were more than that. They were coaches on the floor. They were leaders, and the other players looked up to them and took their cues from them. When a player is also a leader and a coach, the team tends to come together and fly in formation. That's when magic happens.

I think it's significant that each of these players went on to become a successful coach in the NBA. They had a powerful impact on me as an executive. Watching them play, I realized that when players compete so intensely and set an example for their teammates, success happens.

★ ★ ★

Bill Russell

Good Enough Is Never Good Enough

Born in 1934, Bill Russell played center for the Boston Celtics from 1956 to 1969. He was a five-time NBA MVP and a twelve-time all-star, leading the Celtics to eleven NBA championships over his thirteen-year career with the team. He won gold at the 1956 Summer Olympics as captain of the USA basketball team. And I'm proud to say that Russell is my friend. One of the highlights of my broadcasting career was a one-hour live radio interview with him. I'll never forget that show.

I have always been fascinated by the high standards of performance Russell always set for himself. As a player, he used to keep a personal scorecard, and he'd grade his own performance after every game. His scoring system was based on a scale of one to a hundred, with a hundred being perfection. After the best game of Russell's 1,128-game career, he gave himself a mere sixty-five on his personal scorecard. *Sixty-five!*

Why did Russell grade himself so harshly? He did so because his goal was not a "good enough" performance. His goal was not 99 percent. His goal was nothing less than perfection.

Though Russell never reached perfection, he did achieve something that few other people have ever known. He achieved greatness.

★ ★ ★

Joe Falls

"Enjoy Your Life and Be Good to People"

Along with such legends as Ring Lardner, Grantland Rice, and Heywood Campbell Broun, longtime Detroit sportswriter Joe Falls is a member of the Baseball Hall of Fame. Of the many guests I've had on my sports radio show in Orlando, Falls was one of my favorites. Near the end of one interview, he said out of the clear blue sky, "Pat, you want to know the keys to success?"

"I sure do, Joe," I said. "What are they?"

"Two things: enjoy your life and be good to people."

I think about those words often. They're true. Falls lived those words, and he was a success in anybody's book.

★ ★ ★

Amy Grant and Michael Jordan

"Now That Was Fun!"

Every spring, the Arnold Palmer Invitational takes place at Palmer's golf course in Orlando. It's a benefit for the Arnold Palmer Hospital for Children and the Winnie Palmer Hospital. The tournament kicks off with a celebrity round on the first day.

Some years ago, I went as a spectator, along with five thousand other people, and watched a marvelous foursome consisting of Arnold Palmer, NBA legend Michael Jordan, Governor Tom Ridge of Pennsylvania, and Christian pop singer Amy Grant.

Jordan teed off first. Then Palmer. Then Governor Ridge. Grant went last from the women's tee. She hit a beautiful, unbelievable shot that landed on the green. An excited murmur rippled through the crowd as we all moved down the fairway toward the green, where Grant putted to win the first hole.

I stayed as close as I could to Jordan. He's the ultimate competitor, and I wanted to hear his reaction. Sure enough, as he walked to the second hole, I heard him muttering to nobody in particular, "We got us a *game* going here!"

I don't recall how the round finished, but Grant's shot on the first hole and Jordan's reaction are etched in my memory.

Years later, I was in Nashville for a Christmas concert. My daughter Karyn, who is a singer-songwriter, was in the concert along with Amy Grant and was able to get me into the dressing room, where I got to visit with Grant for about twenty minutes.

As we chatted, I said, "Amy, do you recall the Arnold Palmer Invitational in Orlando when you hit that incredible drive on the first hole? I was in the crowd that day, and I'll never forget the look on Michael Jordan's face when he saw your first drive land on the green."

"How could I forget that day?" she said. "Now that was fun!"

★ ★ ★

Max Patkin

A Serious Clown

Max Patkin was known as the "Clown Prince of Baseball"—a title he held for more than five decades. There was nothing he wouldn't do to get a laugh. You might remember him from his role in the hit movie *Bull Durham*.

His biggest crowd-pleaser was shooting water straight up out of his mouth like a human water fountain. I'm not sure exactly how he did it, but I know he had a way of swallowing water and holding it in his gullet. Then, without taking another sip of water, he could tilt his head back and shoot water in the air again and again for the next five minutes, as if he had an inexhaustible supply. Just when you thought he had shot out all the water he had, he'd do it again!

I met Patkin while playing my first professional baseball game in 1962. I had just signed with the Miami Marlins, a class D Phillies farm club in the Florida State League. Our manager, Andy Seminick, put me in the game in left field. My first two times at bat I struck out on six pitches. I thought, *Oh boy, at this rate my career is not going to last long.*

My third at bat didn't start any better. The first two pitches were strikes. So at that point, I had taken eight consecutive pitches, all strikes, either swinging or looking. But I got a hold of the next pitch and drove the ball into right center field for a stand-up double. Oh, sweet relief! What joy!

Coaching third base that inning was the inimitable Max Patkin, who was doing his clown act. The next hitter grounded out, so I bounced on over to third. At that point, Patkin turned all his funny stuff on me. He dragged me off the bag and planted a big kiss on my mouth! It was embarrassing, but the crowd loved it.

Patkin and I became good friends, and our friendship endured through nearly four decades. During my tenure as the general manager of the Spartanburg Phillies, I brought him to town to perform twice a year. When I moved to Philadelphia, I had him perform at 76ers games—a baseball clown entertaining a basketball crowd. When I moved to Orlando, I brought him to town to do his comedy dance act for the Magic fans (he was the greatest jitterbugger in the history of dancing).

I had many conversations with Patkin over the years, and he once explained his simple philosophy of life this way: "I live to make people laugh. They come to the ballpark to enjoy a ballgame, and I'm going to see that they enjoy the game and have a few laughs whether their team wins or not. I don't take myself seriously at all, but I take this job very seriously. When it comes to making people laugh, I'm as serious as they come. I take great pride in making a fool of myself."

Patkin was a beloved figure who brought fun with him wherever he went, and when he passed away in 1999, a great deal of pure, wholesome fun went with him—but I hear there's a lot more laughter in heaven.

★ ★ ★

Pete Rose

A Heart Full of Enthusiasm

Years ago, I was catching in an old-timers' baseball game, and our first baseman was none other than Pete Rose. What a privilege it was to play on the same diamond with the man known as "Charlie Hustle"! He won three World Series rings, three batting titles, and two Gold Gloves, and he made seventeen all-star appearances, playing at five different positions.

My three oldest boys—Jimmy, Bobby, and David—were in their teens, and they got to sit in the dugout during the game. It was a treat for them to rub shoulders with guys they had only seen on television and bubble gum cards. Bobby was on his high school baseball team at the time, so I took him over to Rose and said, "I'd like you to talk to Bobby about hustle. You were synonymous with that word when you played in Cincinnati and Philadelphia, and I'd love to have Bobby hear about hustle straight from you."

Rose looked at Bobby and said, "That's funny, because I never really cared for that nickname 'Charlie Hustle.' I don't think of what I do as hustle. Instead, I like the word *enthusiasm*. I went out there and had so much fun doing my job that I just had to do it well. The way I see it, Bobby, is that God gave me certain skills—not great skills but good skills. You can't make it in this game on good skills alone. But if you take the skills God gave you at birth and you add an intense desire and great enthusiasm, you just might have a special career.

"Bobby, there has not been a day of my baseball career that I didn't step onto the field with a heart full of enthusiasm. I was excited to be at the ballpark every day, and once I got there, I couldn't wait to hear 'Play ball!' I always had a ton of fun playing baseball. That's what it's all about."

Bobby never forgot those words—and neither have I.

★ ★ ★

Sandy Koufax

"Enjoy the Whole Experience"

For years, the great Dodgers left-handed pitcher Sandy Koufax has lived a quiet, private life in Vero Beach, Florida. Though famed for his stellar achievements on the mound (including a perfect game on September 9, 1965, three Cy Young Awards, and four World Series championships), Koufax is a big basketball fan. He played basketball in college, and some have said he was an even better basketball player than a pitcher in those days.

In 1995, when the Orlando Magic were in the NBA finals, I received a message from Koufax saying that he wanted to come up and attend the game. So I got him tickets and took him down to our locker room.

As we chatted, I learned that Koufax had started running marathons. "Well, you and I are in the same boat," I said. "I'm getting ready to run my first marathon. What advice can you give me? What can you tell me about running marathons that I may not already know?"

"Let me tell you four things," he said. "First, don't go out too fast. Second, drink water at every station. You've got to stay hydrated. Third, enjoy the whole experience. It's meant to be fun, so go out and enjoy it. Fourth, if you go out to dinner that night after the marathon, make sure you don't have to go down any stairs. Your legs are going to be so rubbery that you'll never navigate those stairs."

I've always remembered his advice—especially the part about having fun. Yes, a marathon is long, punishing, grueling, and exhausting, but if you go into it with the right attitude, a marathon is also fun. "Enjoy the whole experience," Koufax told me. I carried that advice in my heart every mile, and I try to remember it every day.

★ ★ ★

Mike Krzyzewski

Watching Film at Five A.M.

After six seasons with the Detroit Pistons, Grant Hill came to Orlando and played seven seasons with the Magic. I came to know him as a young man of exceptional character. In college, Grant played for Coach Mike Krzyzewski at Duke. Grant told me how he learned the importance of preparation as an ingredient of success.

"When I was an eighteen-year-old freshman," he said, "I broke my nose very badly in a game in December. Coach K invited me to stay in his home over Christmas break. Because I had so much pain from my broken nose, I had a lot of trouble sleeping. I'd wake up and couldn't go back to sleep. So I'd come out of my room at four or five in the morning, and every time I came out, Coach K was already up!

I found out that he got up early every morning and watched game film of our next opponent. That spoke volumes to me about the way he prepared for each game. Whenever I'm tempted to slack off, I remember Coach K watching game film at five in the morning."

★ ★ ★

Bill Walton

"Prepare Yourself Mentally for Anything"

In a lecture at the University of Lille, December 7, 1854, French biologist Louis Pasteur said, "*Le hasard ne favorise que les esprits préparés.*" In case you couldn't understand my accent, here's the English translation: "Fortune favors only the prepared mind." Abraham Lincoln made a similar observation using a woodsman's metaphor: "Give me six hours to chop down a tree and I will spend the first four hours sharpening my axe."

One man who agrees with those sentiments is former UCLA and NBA basketball star Bill Walton. As a guest on my radio show, he once said, "I love the pressure and anticipation of the game. I love the preparation and practice. When I was at UCLA, Coach John Wooden taught us to love the process of getting ready for a game. He said that you build good game habits by the way you prepare yourself ahead of time.

"You prepare yourself mentally for anything that might happen in the game. You visualize the game a thousand times in your mind before it happens. As you rehearse your game plan in practice, you get into a flow with your teammates. You memorize all of their moves so that you begin to move in sync with them. Through repetition, your body and your mind memorize all the moves. Then, in the game, everything becomes automatic, like pushing a button."

Or, to put it more simply, "*Le hasard ne favorise que les esprits préparés.*"

★ ★ ★

Bobby Bowden

A Sixty-to-One Ratio

Bobby Bowden, longtime football coach of the Florida State Seminoles, told me he once calculated that he and his assistants spent at least one full hour of planning and preparation for each minute his players were on the football field. That works out to a sixty-to-one ratio of prep time to playing time.

"I have always gotten my greatest pleasure," he once said, "out of breaking down film, learning about opponents, then implementing a game plan to take advantage of our strengths and their weaknesses. I love to take a group of young men in the late summer and mold them into a team."

Bowden's love of strategic preparation goes back to 1943. He was a sports-obsessed thirteen-year-old when he came down with rheumatic fever and was forced to spend more than a year confined at home (including six months of bed rest). His source of entertainment in those pre-television days was the radio. "I basically listened to a play-by-play of World War II for a year," he said. In his imagination, young Bowden pictured the battlefield terrain, the placement of troops and tanks, and the strategic movement of those forces. He didn't realize it then, but he was preparing himself for a lifetime of coaching football.

His long career is a testimony to the power of preparation.

★ ★ ★

David Stern

An Extra Set of Ears

In 1986, we were petitioning the NBA to grant an expansion franchise in Orlando—the franchise that would become the Orlando Magic. We were at a point where we had to make a deposit of one hundred thousand dollars to prove to the league that we were legit. So I led a delegation to the New York City office of NBA commissioner David Stern.

At the time, Miami and Tampa were considered the odds-on favorites for expansion. Orlando was a smaller city without a major airport and without an arena. Our bid was clearly a long shot, so our little group had a lot of convincing to do.

I wanted to create a visual symbol that would be splashed across the sports pages of the nation, a symbol that would say to the world, "The NBA belongs in Orlando!" And what better symbol of Orlando could there be than a set of Mickey Mouse ears from Walt Disney World?

For the life of me, I don't know why I came prepared with not one but *two* sets of mouse ears. Perhaps I had a premonition, or perhaps I simply had a vague feeling that a second set of mouse ears might come in handy. In any case, I came prepared.

We had a huge media turnout for the event. I stood alongside Commissioner Stern for the photo opportunity and handed him the check for a hundred grand. As we posed for the pictures, I pulled out a set of mouse ears and plopped them on Stern's head.

He immediately yanked them off, but I was ready for that. I pulled out the second set of ears and plopped them on his head. He couldn't move fast enough to remove the second pair, and that's when all the flashbulbs popped. The picture of Stern wearing Mickey Mouse ears went out all over the country. It gave an added boost to our nationwide publicity campaign and helped tilt the odds for success in our favor.

I had gotten my wish. Magic was in the air.

Fast-forward almost three decades. In January 2014, I was interviewing Stern on my radio show. He was approaching retirement after thirty years as NBA commissioner, and he was very relaxed. We had a great conversation, and I asked him to reflect on the period of expansion and what it meant to the league.

He talked about the expansion era, about the rise in interest in pro basketball, about the great players that came into the league, and about the excitement of the fans. "It was an exciting time," he concluded, "to be the commissioner of the NBA—in spite of the fact that you tricked me and put those Mickey Mouse ears on my head!"

Ha! He hadn't forgotten!

★ ★ ★

Alex Martins

There's No Such Thing as a Sure Thing

The 1992 NBA draft lottery was one of the most significant in the annals of the league. Whoever won the number one pick was assured of drafting a once-in-a-lifetime player: Shaquille O'Neal. The lottery was held at the NBA Films headquarters in New Jersey. All eleven teams that failed to make the play-offs took part in the lottery.

NBC broadcaster Bob Costas was emceeing the event and would be interviewing the representative of the lottery-winning team. So I went to him and said, "Bob, keep my seat warm up there. I'll be talking to you right after the lottery."

The ceremony commenced. The Magic had the worst record in the league, so we were allowed ten of the sixty-six Ping-Pong balls in the lottery machine. Commissioner David Stern officiated, and a representative from a major accounting firm was on hand to certify the fairness of the lottery. The doors of the room were locked. No one could go in or out until the ceremony was completed.

The results of the bouncing Ping-Pong balls were indicated by an arrangement of cards with team logos printed on them. As the network cameras recorded the event, Commissioner Stern turned over the cards one by one, revealing the logos of the teams in ascending order, from eleventh to first. As each logo was revealed, the suspense was excruciating.

By the time Stern reached the second from the last card, only two logos were left to be revealed—the Charlotte Hornets and the Orlando Magic. Stern turned the second from the last card faceup. The Hornets had gotten the second pick! The Magic card was still facedown! We had won the lottery!

I was numb as I rose from my seat and went to the podium to be congratulated by Stern. I held up our Magic Shaq jersey, and the cameras captured my look of stunned amazement.

Moments later, I sat down next to Bob Costas for an interview. "Pat Williams," he said, "you told me before the lottery to keep your chair warm because you were going to be back here to talk about winning the first pick—and here you are."

And there I was!

We had won the first pick, and drafting Shaq looked like a sure thing. But the draft was still five weeks away, and we were about to discover that there's no such thing as a sure thing.

The draft is normally held in New York City, but because of the World Games that year, the draft was held in Portland, Oregon. All the players in the draft, including Shaq, had to be in Portland to be introduced on national television.

About ten thousand Magic fans were in our arena for the event. I stood on a platform in the center of the arena so the fans could see me in person while watching the draft live from Portland on our giant screens. We had a high-tech satellite phone hookup that had been tested and double-checked. All I had to do was pick up the phone and announce that Orlando was selecting Shaquille O'Neal of LSU.

What could go wrong?

At the appointed time, I picked up the phone, smiled to the crowd, and heard—nothing. No dial tone. The line was dead.

I looked around for help. The technical wizards whispered, "Try it again!" I did. The line was still dead. I began to sweat. Panic rose.

I realized that we had no contingency plan for a technology breakdown. We should have instructed our people in Portland, "If anything goes wrong, just take Shaq!" But we hadn't prepared for this.

An anxious murmur spread through the crowd. Our fans were wondering why I was just standing there, grinning foolishly and sweating buckets. The clock was ticking. If we didn't get word to Portland in the next few seconds, we would forfeit our number one pick!

Then I saw the Magic's ace publicity director (now CEO) Alex Martins calmly dialing his cell phone. "Tell Commissioner Stern," he said calmly, "we're taking Shaquille O'Neal of LSU." Moments later, Stern announced our selection on national television.

For years afterward, I had nightmares about that event. I would wake up in a cold sweat, recalling the draft pick that almost didn't happen because we failed to prepare for a high-tech snafu. Being prepared for crises is a key to success. I'll always be grateful that Alex Martins was calm, competent, and prepared that day.

★ ★ ★
Johnny Kelley

"Don't Go Out Too Fast"

John Adelbert Kelley was probably the most famous Boston Marathoner of all time. He competed in his first Boston Marathon in 1928 and ran his last full Boston Marathon in 1992 at the age of eighty-four. He finished fifty-eight Boston Marathons in his lifetime and competed in the Olympics in 1936 and 1948. A statue of Johnny Kelley stands near city hall in Newton, Massachusetts.

I ran the first of my thirteen Boston Marathons in 1996, while Kelley was still living but after he had given up marathon running. He was a beloved figure and a legend around the city of Boston.

On Sunday before the event, he'd always be at Fenway Park to throw out the first pitch before the Red Sox game. The fans, all thirty-five thousand of them, would go crazy when he came out. In his later years, he wasn't able to throw the ball over home plate, but nobody booed him. They'd boo anybody else, but they didn't boo Johnny Kelley.

On the day of the marathon, I would eat breakfast around 6:30, and there would be Kelley talking with all the anxious runners, including me. We would all gather around him, seeking his counsel.

I'd say, "What advice do you have for someone like me?"

His advice was always the same, yet I loved to hear it. "Don't go out too fast," he'd say. "It'll come back to bite you. Don't get caught up too early. Pace yourself. Those hills at the end of the race will kill you if you don't."

I was always thrilled to be in Kelley's presence. I was honored to listen to him, to learn from him, and to follow—literally—in his footsteps.

★ ★ ★

John F. Kennedy

Even Charisma Can Be Learned

When my sister Ruthie was a high school senior in Wilmington, Delaware, a Massachusetts senator named John F. Kennedy was running for president. My parents were lifelong Democrats, and Mom just adored JFK. So when the Democratic Party of Delaware held a major fund-raiser in Kennedy's honor, Mom was front and center.

The dinner was held at the Scottish Rite Cathedral in Wilmington, and Mom and Dad took Ruthie with them. My mother was bold and knew no fear, so before JFK gave his speech, Mom took Ruthie in tow and went right up to Senator Kennedy for a chat. She introduced Ruthie and explained to the senator that she had been accepted to Vassar and would be attending classes there in the fall.

Ruthie was completely bedazzled by Senator Kennedy's charm. She recently told me that she still remembers that encounter like it was yesterday. They chatted briefly, then Mom and Ruthie returned to their table.

Since it was a school night, Mom asked a friend of the family to drive Ruthie home. As Ruthie and the family friend slipped out a side entrance to head for the parking lot, they saw another door open at the same time. Kennedy and some of his aides and handlers were slipping out at the same time.

Ruthie stared as the future president strode to his limousine. As he was about to enter the car, Kennedy spotted Ruthie across the dark parking lot. He smiled at her and said (in his trademark Boston accent), "Good luck at Vassah!"

My sister has never gotten over that moment. Kennedy greeted her and even remembered where she was going to attend college. As Ruthie told me not long ago, "I was thrilled then, and I'm still thrilled whenever I remember it. I have his picture on my refrigerator, and I've loved him ever since."

Kennedy had a quality called charm or charisma. Many people assume that charisma is a natural gift—you're either born with it or you're not. I challenge that assumption. I'm convinced that practically every desirable trait can be learned and acquired: leadership ability, speaking ability, strong work ethic, boldness, and, yes, even charisma. I believe we can boost our own charisma by focusing on a few simple skills: making good eye contact, smiling with confidence, projecting an attitude of enthusiasm, listening to others and remembering some key details about them, leaning into the conversation, and remaining humble and gracious. These are all learnable skills, and I believe JFK studied and learned them.

Historians say that, as a young man, John F. Kennedy was painfully awkward and self-conscious. But when Kennedy was in his early twenties, he underwent a personal transformation. In *The Kennedys: An American Drama*, Peter Collier and David Horowitz note that Kennedy had a friend, Chuck Spaulding, who was an assistant to actor Gary Cooper. Spaulding took Kennedy around prewar Hollywood and introduced him to many film stars. Spaulding later said that Kennedy "was very interested in that binding magnetism these screen personalities had. What exactly was it? How did you go about acquiring it?"[1]

When my sister Ruthie was captivated by that fabled Kennedy charisma, she couldn't have imagined that it was a skill he had acquired while observing screen stars like Gary Cooper and Clark Gable. She just knew that she had been charmed, and JFK's charisma still lives in my sister's memory fifty years after the gleam of Camelot died.

★ ★ ★

Larry Bowa

"If Every Game Is Like This One"

It was opening day 1966, and the Greenville Mets had come to Duncan Park to play the Spartanburg Phillies. I was the Phillies' twenty-five-year-old general manager. Our nineteen-year-old rookie shortstop, Larry Bowa, was our leadoff hitter, and the Greenville Mets' pitcher struck him out on three pitches.

In the course of the game, Bowa came up to bat three more times—and struck out three more times. In his pro debut, Larry Bowa was 0-4 with four strikeouts. Not exactly an auspicious start.

That night, Bowa called his dad, a former ballplayer and manager who lived in California. "Dad," he said, "if every game is like this one, I'll be coming home soon."

What Bowa didn't realize was that the Mets pitcher who struck him out was a young flamethrower named Nolan Ryan, who would go on to have a twenty-seven-year Hall of Fame career in baseball—a career that included seven no-hitters, three more than any other pitcher in Major League Baseball history.

Though Larry Bowa's first game in pro baseball seemed a bad omen, he didn't let a rough start keep him down. He battled back and went on to enjoy a long career in baseball (he is currently the Philadelphia Phillies' bench coach).

★ ⭐ ★

John Havlicek

"Obstacles Are More Mental than Physical"

John Havlicek is widely recognized as one of the greatest basketball players of all time. He played sixteen seasons with the Boston Celtics, won eight NBA titles, and was inducted into the Basketball Hall of Fame in 1984. I once had him on my radio show, and I asked him if perseverance was a big factor in his successful career.

"Perseverance is absolutely important," he replied. "The obstacles you face are more mental than physical. When two people play against each other, the question is who will give up first. It becomes a mental game of one-on-one. The object is to see who is mentally tougher—you or the other guy—on every single move, on every individual shot.

"The player who wins is the one who works a little harder, who goes a little longer. I believe you will pass out before you are overworked, but most people don't know that. They think they're overworked, so they stop. They could have kept going, but they didn't. They weren't beaten physically. They were beaten mentally. Those who persevere win."

Havlicek announced that he was retiring after the 1978 season, so when he came to Philadelphia to play his last game in the Spectrum Arena, we honored him with a tribute before the game. Even though he played for our perennial rivals, the Celtics, it was an emotional ceremony for our hometown fans, and Havlicek was clearly touched. On April 12, 1978, he sent me a handwritten note that read:

> *Dear Pat,*
>
> *I want to take the time to thank you for the wonderful pregame ceremony on my last trip to the Spectrum.*
>
> *The gifts, the crowd, the gestures, and the hospitality of you and your organization made it a most memorable affair, and I'm most appreciative.*
>
> *John Havlicek*

A very classy word of thanks from the great John Havlicek.

★ ★ ★

Barry Manilow

"I'll Do Anything to Get People to Hear My Music"

In October 1974, when I was the general manager of the Philadelphia 76ers, I was working on a fall-themed promotion for an upcoming game with the Knicks. We had all kinds of activities planned—bobbing for apples, a pumpkin-pie-eating contest, treats for the kids, and on and on. While I was trying to manage all the details, my phone rang. It was Barry Abrams, a record promoter who worked part-time at our games.

"Pat," he said, "could you do me a favor? I'm working with a terrific young recording artist who has a new song. Could you play it at the game tonight?"

"I don't know, Barry," I said. "That's not the kind of thing we usually do. Plus, I'm up to my ears with this new promotion."

"You'd be doing me a huge favor."

I sighed. "Okay, have him bring me his tape before the game. I'll see what I can do." I hung up and forgot all about it.

An hour before the game, a lanky, long-haired young man approached me and said, "Mr. Williams? Barry Abrams said I should see you. I brought my tape." He held out a cassette.

It took me a moment to recall my chat with Abrams. "Oh, yeah. Are you sure you want to play your song in this arena? The acoustics are terrible."

"Mr. Williams," he said, "I'll take my tapes to sporting events, radio stations, school dances, birthday parties, bar mitzvahs—anyplace at all. I'll do anything to get people to hear my music, because if they hear it, they'll like it."

I told him to take his tape to Joe the sound guy up in the glass booth. "Tell Joe that anything you want is okay with me." Then I went back to work.

Sometime later, the arena filled with fans, the 76ers and Knicks took the court, and the game got underway. During a time-out, I noticed a song playing over the public address system—a smooth, plaintive love ballad. When the song ended, a smattering of applause broke out in the stands. Well, somebody out there liked the kid's music.

I didn't think any more about it until the next time I heard that song. It was playing on the radio—and it was a huge hit. The song was "Mandy," the breakthrough recording that launched the career of a young singer-songwriter named Barry Manilow.

★ ★ ★

Martin Luther King Jr.

"Nothing Ever Rattled Him"

In the summer of 2012, former CBS anchorman Dan Rather came on my radio show to talk about his new book *Rather Outspoken*. He was effusive and eager to talk. I was especially interested in his thoughts on Martin Luther King Jr.

As the Southern bureau chief for CBS news during the most turbulent years of the civil rights movement, Rather had covered

King almost daily and had interviewed him a number of times. Rather vividly recalled what many people now forget—that King endured searing hatred, death threats, and actual violence throughout those years of conflict and opposition.

"King was not a perfect man," Rather told me, "but he was a courageous man with a vision for a better America. He risked everything and worked tirelessly for that vision, and he succeeded in breaking the back of institutional segregation in America."

I asked Rather for a personal assessment of King's character. "King," he said, "was a self-contained man, but he had the ability to connect with people of all different stripes. Bill Clinton had the same quality. Both men, regardless of how busy they were, would stop what they were doing and give you their full attention. They were there in the moment with you. Dr. King was under constant pressure, tension, and chaos, but nothing ever rattled him. The more intense his circumstances, the steadier he got. I like to say that he was quiet at the center."

★ ★ ★

Pat Robertson

"I Thought I Could Win"

I've gotten to know Christian television host Pat Robertson through my many appearances on *The 700 Club*. I go on the show about once a year to promote a new book, and Robertson is always very kind to me. He has invited me to Regent University on four occasions to speak.

One time, several years ago, I gave the commencement address. Afterward, I shed the cap and gown I had been wearing on that ninety-degree day and had lunch with Robertson. Over lunch, I reminisced with him about the 1988 presidential primaries. He entered the primaries, finished second in Iowa (ahead of President George H. W. Bush), and won the majority of delegates in the Washington State caucus. But he was not much of a factor in the multiple-state primaries. Still, it was an audacious attempt by a political outsider to take on a sitting president.

I asked Robertson what prompted him to enter the race. He looked at me as if I had just asked the silliest question ever uttered.

He said, "Because I thought I could win."

★ ★ ★

Stan Musial

"Ever Have a Day Like That?"

All the great stars of baseball came out to the 1992 grand opening of the Ted Williams Museum and Hitters Hall of Fame. One of those stars was one of Ted Williams's contemporaries, Stan Musial, who played twenty-two seasons (1941 through 1963) with the St. Louis Cardinals. Nicknamed "Stan the Man," Musial is universally acknowledged as one of the greatest hitters in Major League Baseball history. He was certainly one of the most consistent hitters in baseball, with 1,815 career hits at home and exactly the same number of career hits on the road. His record of 3,630 career hits ranks fourth over-all and first among players who spent their entire career with one team.

I enjoyed getting to talk to Musial during the museum event, and he told me a story from his playing days that says a lot about his confidence as a player. "I was in the locker room one day," he said, "and a rookie came in and said, 'I feel great! I think I'm gonna get three hits today! You ever have a day like that, Stan?' I said, 'Yeah. Every day.'"

★ ★ ★

Jack Youngblood

No Regrets

How tough do you have to be to play football on a broken leg? On December 30, 1979, LA Rams defensive end Jack Youngblood was in Dallas playing in a divisional play-off game against the Cowboys. Late in the second quarter, two Dallas offensive linemen chop-blocked him, leaving him writhing in pain. The Rams' trainers carted him off to the locker room, where the doctor X-rayed his leg. The picture showed that his calf bone had snapped a couple of inches above the ankle.

"Tape up my leg," Youngblood demanded, "and bring me some aspirin!"

The doctor protested, but Youngblood insisted—and he prevailed. He went back into the game and even managed to sack Roger Staubach on a key play. The Rams upset the Cowboys 21-19.

Youngblood played the next game, the NFC championship game in Tampa Bay, with a plastic cast on his leg. The Rams beat Tampa Bay 9-0 for the NFC title.

In Super Bowl XIV in Pasadena, the Rams faced Terry Bradshaw and the Pittsburgh Steelers. Once again, Youngblood played the entire game with a broken bone in his leg.

Near the end of the game, the Rams were ahead and the Steelers were mired deep in their own territory. On third and eight, Bradshaw took the snap, faked a handoff, and stepped back to throw. Youngblood blew through the line and barreled straight for Bradshaw, who was waiting for his receiver to get open downfield. Youngblood was just a half step too late. Bradshaw unleashed the pass, and the receiver caught the ball and took it to the end zone for a seventy-three-yard touchdown.

The Steelers won, but Youngblood had no regrets playing in the Super Bowl on a broken leg. "The only regret I would have had," he later said, "is if I hadn't played."

Today, Youngblood lives in Orlando and is actively involved in many organizations, including the Orlando chapter of the Christian organization Young Life. I see him from time to time, and I've told him I have to admire a guy who has the guts to chase down Roger Staubach and Terry Bradshaw on a broken leg.

★ ★ ★

Kevin Garnett

"Focus! Focus! Focus!"

Some years ago, the Boston Celtics came to our arena to play the Magic. It was around the midpoint of the season, and the two teams had nearly identical records. The game was going to be televised nationally, so the pressure was intense.

More than an hour before the game, I went down to the visiting team's locker room to talk to the Celtics' power forward Kevin Garnett. I wanted to give him a signed copy of my most recent book and ask him to autograph his picture on the new Wheaties box so we could auction it for charity.

I found Garnett sitting in a chair, staring off into space while a trainer taped his ankles. The look on his face was intimidating. You've heard the expression "He has his game face on." Well, until you see Kevin Garnett's game face, you don't know what that term really means. His eyes were intense and fierce. His jaw was set like stone. I could actually feel an emotional aura around him, like static electricity before a thunderstorm.

Garnett was in a zone all his own. I found his demeanor so intimidating that I wanted to take my book and my Wheaties box and just get outta there! But I gulped hard, summoned my courage, and said, "Uh, Kevin, I'd like you to sign this Wheaties box for charity."

"Mr. Williams," Kevin said, glancing at me as if noticing me for the first time, "I don't *sign* anything, I don't *look* at anything, I don't *do* anything before a game."

He raised his right hand up before his face, holding it like an ax with the blade aimed straight in front of him. Then he slowly chopped the air with his hand. "Focus! Focus! Focus!" he said. "Before the game, I don't want any distractions. After the game, I'll sign the box. Right now, I'm focused on the game."

Then his face again became a mask of intense concentration. I had often heard of Garnett's intensity as a player, but until I saw him in the locker room that night, I had no idea what that really meant.

"Focus! Focus! Focus!" That's why Kevin Garnett is a champion.

★ ★ ★

Paul Hornung and Jerry West

The "Focus" Switch

My friend Ernie Accorsi, former New York Giants general manager, played in a celebrity golf tournament with retired Hall of Fame running back Paul Hornung, who played for Vince Lombardi's Green Bay Packers from 1957 through 1966. Hornung is a colorful cowboy-type guy who speaks with a laid-back Kentucky drawl. For most of the round, Hornung had been playing in an easygoing manner that matched his drawl.

But as they moved into the final six holes, Hornung and his companions realized they had a chance to win the tournament. Accorsi told me, "I've never seen a switch go on like I saw the switch go on in Paul Hornung. He turned on the 'focus' switch, and all the funny stuff and kidding around were gone. He stopped laughing, and it was just pure focus for the last six holes. And we won! Hornung carried us, and I got to see a world-class athlete do something only a world-class athlete can do. I saw him turn on the 'focus' switch."

Another world-class athlete who exemplifies the "focus" switch is legendary basketball star Jerry West, who retired in 1974 after a fourteen-year career with the Los Angeles Lakers. He has also been a head coach and general manager with the Lakers. West is so closely identified with NBA basketball that the NBA logo incorporates his silhouette for its distinctive image.

I was at a store in Orlando doing a book signing when a man approached me and asked, "How well do you know Jerry West?"

"We've been in this business a long time together," I replied. "I know Jerry pretty well. Why do you ask?"

"I played golf with him one day," the gentleman told me, "and it's not much fun playing golf with Jerry. He's so intense, so focused, that it's hard to have fun around him. You oughta see this guy putt. He's a great putter, but it's all business with him. Nothing deters him; nothing distracts him. You can't speak to him. He's totally focused on his game."

Yes, that described West all right, but that's the key to his success over the years. He approached basketball the same way he approached golf—with an intense, unbreakable focus. He turned on that "focus" switch, and nothing could keep him from his goal.

I remember bringing West to Orlando in 1986, when we were trying to bring an NBA franchise to town. West spoke at a rally to stir up the community to get behind the Magic, and his presence gave a huge boost to our efforts. After West spoke, we had a Q&A session, and someone asked him if, out of all the thousands of games he'd played, any games stood out in his mind.

"Well," West said, "I remember one game when I was eighteen for twenty from the floor and twelve for twelve from the free throw line, and I had a 103-degree fever." And he went on to describe some memorable moments from that game.

Could you deliver one of your best performances with a 103-degree fever? West could flip the "focus" switch and completely block out his fever, the distractions from the crowd, and the pressure, and he could shoot eighteen of twenty from the floor and twelve of twelve from the free throw line. West could put on mental blinders and focus totally on winning. That's what made him great.

★ ★ ★

Michael Jordan

"That's the Jordan Way"

In the late 1990s, the Magic acquired veteran guard B. J. Armstrong, who had played with Michael Jordan and the Bulls during their championship era. On one occasion, I sat next to Armstrong on the team bus and told him about my book project on Jordan. "Take a look at my outline for the book," I said. "I've tried to list all the character qualities that have made Michael so successful. What do you think, B. J.? Did I capture the man?"

"It looks pretty good," he said, reading through the outline, "except for one thing. In fact, you've forgotten the most important thing that makes Michael who he is."

The most important thing? What had I missed?

"B. J.," I said, "I'm all ears."

"Focus," he said. "That's what sets Michael apart. He has an almost superhuman ability to be in the moment, totally focused on his goal. His concentration is absolute. His head is totally in the game—no distractions. Nothing interferes with his focus. That's what sets him apart."

Armstrong was right. I had totally missed that key element of Jordan's greatness. Just a few months after my conversation with Armstrong, the focus factor was underscored for me once again.

I had written to veteran NBC newsman Tim Russert, the host of *Meet the Press*. I knew that Russert had interviewed Jordan on television a number of times, so I asked him if he could share with me the secret of Jordan's success as an athlete and competitor. Russert replied at Christmastime with a handwritten note.

Dear Pat,

Focus. Focus. Focus. Then get it done. That's the Jordan way.

Have a nice holiday.

Tim Russert

* ★ *

Don Shula

"You Were Completely Focused"

After Don Shula retired as the head coach of the Miami Dolphins, the longtime coach sat in the stands with his friend

Charlie Morgan to watch a Dolphins game for the first time as a mere spectator.

Between the third and fourth quarters, the team owner's wife came out and honored some inner-city kids in a brief ceremony near the Dolphins' bench. Shula was impressed. "What a great idea!" he said. "How long has that been going on?"

"Don," Charlie replied, "they did that at every home game throughout your entire coaching career."

Shula was astounded. "I never knew that!"

"Of course you didn't," Charlie replied. "You were completely focused on the game."

★ ★ ★

Carol Channing and Mary Martin

Never Retire

In the summer of 1986, three cities were competing hard to obtain an NBA expansion franchise in Florida—Miami, Tampa, and Orlando. The Miami effort was headed by Zev Buffman, an Israeli-born Broadway impresario with strong Florida ties and more than forty Broadway productions to his credit. So, for a while, Buffman and I were intense rivals.

Once the word came down that the NBA had selected *both* Orlando and Miami for expansion franchises, the rivalry subsided, and Buffman and I became friends. In fact, it wasn't long after the league made its decision that Buffman called me and invited me to attend a new stage show that was coming to Orlando costarring Carol Channing and Mary Martin. "Come see the show," he said. "Afterward I'm hosting Carol and Mary at dinner, and we'd like you and your wife to join us."

I had grown up loving the theater. My mother had taken my sisters and me to New York for many Broadway shows, and I had seen Carol onstage in *Hello, Dolly!* and Mary in *South Pacific*. Getting to see them on the same stage together, then have dinner with them, would be the experience of a lifetime.

So we went to the show. It was a comedy called *Legends* by James Kirkwood Jr., and it told the story of two rival film stars late in their careers. It was funny, warm, and touching. Carol and Mary were amazing in it, and it seemed to have been written expressly for them.

After the show, we met Buffman and the two stars for dinner, and it was as if the show went into extra acts! For ninety minutes, it was impossible to get a word in edgewise between Carol and Mary. But why would I want to talk when it was so fascinating to listen? These two ladies had so much theater history in common, and they shared gossip, tall tales, and reminiscences without end. I hung on every word.

It occurred to me that, even though Carol and Mary were no longer onstage, they were still performing, still entertaining, still pleasing the audience. In fact, they were practically still in character! Because *Legends* was about two longtime actresses, it was hard to say where the character began and the actress left off.

One of my takeaways from that evening was the realization that when you love what you do, you never want to stop, you never want to retire, you want to keep doing what you love. Even over dinner.

★ ✯ ★

Les Paul

Keep Doing What You Love

When I was growing up in the 1950s, the music was fantastic. One of the great musical innovators of that era was guitarist Les Paul. More than a musician, he was an inventor and instrument designer who pioneered the development of the solid-body electric guitar and helped invent the sound we know as rock 'n' roll. While recording with his wife, Mary Ford, he was one of the first to experiment with overdubbing, multitrack recording, and electronic sound effects. Les Paul and Mary Ford produced some of the most distinctive recordings of that time.

Mary Ford died in 1977, but Les Paul continued performing well into his nineties. A few years ago, my son Jimmy, who lives and works in New York, called me and said, "Dad, I know you like Les Paul. Well, there's a nightclub here where he performs, and I can get us in."

"Jimmy," I said, "I would love that."

So Jimmy got us into the club. The place was packed and turning people away at the doors, but we were able to get seats close to the stage. The lights dimmed and out walked ninety-three-year-old Les Paul. He performed his patented licks and trills on the magical strings and frets of a guitar he himself invented—and then he did a second show later that night.

In August 2009, about three months after we saw him perform, I picked up the paper and read that he had passed away. Though he was gone, he had left us his music—and he had left us a message through the example of his life: Don't retire. Don't let them put you out to pasture. Keep doing what you love until you draw your last breath.

★ ⋆ ★

Bob Feller

The Full Sixty Feet

After retiring from the American League, Hall of Famer Bob Feller played every year in the alumni game. He'd suit up in an Indians uniform, pitch the first inning, then go up into the stands and sign autographs. He did this right up until the end of his life.

In 2006, when he was eighty-eight years old, Feller was playing in one of these alumni games. I was catching for the National League, and our pitcher was Gaylord Perry, another Hall of Famer. Feller and Perry were both pitching pretty well for a couple of old-timers. Feller got some hitters out, and he received a wonderful ovation from an appreciative crowd.

After the game, I was in the clubhouse, and I found Feller sitting at a table signing baseballs. I said, "Bob, that was marvelous. You and Gaylord were the stars of the evening."

Feller said, "Yeah, but I pitched from the full sixty feet."

In other words, Feller claimed that Perry had moved up a few feet in front of the rubber to get the ball over the plate. I hadn't noticed that, but Feller sure did. He had a real competitor's spirit and pride in craftsmanship. Though pushing ninety, he was still competing against a rival pitcher!

★ ★ ★

Satchel Paige

Keep Pitching

In 1965, I was in Spartanburg, trying every which way to promote our team and get people into the ballpark. One day, I was on the phone with my mentor, the great Bill Veeck, and I said, "Bill, is there any way you could get Satchel Paige to come in here and pitch in our ballpark? I'd love to build a promotion around him."

"Let me check," he said. "I'll get back to you."

Satchel Paige was known for his blazing fastball. Joe DiMaggio once said that Paige was the best pitcher he ever faced, and Bob Feller called him the best pitcher he'd ever seen. I knew that Veeck had brought Paige to the major leagues in 1948 and was very close to him. If anyone could reach him, it was Bill Veeck. Soon my phone rang, and it was Veeck. "Yeah," he said, "I can get him there for you. He'll do whatever you want for the promotion."

We advertised that we were bringing in ace right-hander and future Hall of Famer Satchel Paige to pitch against the Spartanburg Phillies. I knew the game had the potential to be a huge crowd-pleaser.

Though Paige was about sixty, he could still pitch, still get guys out, still wow the crowd. He pitched against our guys for three innings in an exhibition, and the promotion was a huge success. Before he left, he signed a photo for me with this inscription: "To Pat Williams from Satchel Paige, who would love to pitch in Spartanburg!" I still have that picture on my wall as a reminder to keep living every day to the fullest—and to keep pitching.

★ ★ ★

Kenny Rogers

"The Very Best I've Got"

I first encountered Kenny Rogers in Philadelphia when I was the general manager of the 76ers. Rogers was a huge star in the 1980s, and he was doing a concert at our arena, which was completely packed. There was a meet-and-greet event with Rogers before the concert, and I was invited. Rogers was glad-handing everyone and getting his picture taken with people right up until an announcement came over the public address system: "Mr. Rogers, you're on in sixty seconds."

With that, he waved good-bye and took off toward the tunnel leading to the stage. I found it amazing that he could switch gears so fast. One minute he's schmoozing, and the next minute he's leaping onto the stage to give a show-stopping performance.

The music blares, the lights play across the stage, the audience roars, and he's on!

Now, fast-forward more than a decade. Sometime after our family moved to Orlando, Rogers did a concert on the campus of the University of Central Florida. The crowd was not as big as in earlier years, but he still had a lot of fans, and he still put on a rousing good show.

Our family attended the meet-and-greet event before the concert, and my wife and I had pictures taken with him. As we were standing next to him, I said, "Kenny, does all of this ever get old? What drives you to keep performing, to keep giving audiences so much energy onstage?"

"The people do," he said. "The moment I hear the music and see the crowd, I think, *These people paid a lot of money to see me get up and perform. I need to give them their money's worth, the very best I've got.* That's what keeps me going."

Part 2

★ ★ ★

Leadership

Walt Disney

Committed to Excellence

In August 1989, three months before the Magic opened its first season, I attended a reception and dinner at one of the Disney hotels in Orlando. I sat next to Dick Nunis, who was then head of Disney Attractions. Nunis had begun his career at Disneyland in 1955, soon after his graduation from USC. He worked alongside Walt Disney for many years and knew him well. So I asked him, "What were the traits of Walt Disney that made him so successful?" Then I grabbed a napkin and scribbled down everything Nunis said.

"You can chalk up Walt Disney's success to nine character traits," Nunis began. "First, integrity—you could absolutely trust the man. Second, creativity—he was a true visionary. Third, administrative ability—he knew how to get the best out of people. Fourth, motivational ability—Walt was not easy to work for, but he could inspire you to perform at a higher level than you ever dreamed possible. Fifth, he was willing to take risks—not reckless gambles but bold, calculated, carefully planned risks. Sixth, Walt was a good listener—he was eager to learn from anyone, including janitors and secretaries. Seventh, he wanted people to challenge him. Eighth, he did his homework—he examined all decisions from every conceivable vantage point."

"And ninth?" I asked.

"That's the most important trait of all. Walt was fanatically committed to excellence. He was a stickler for getting every detail just right. Everything he did had his name on it, so it all had to be top quality."

To underscore his point about quality, Nunis told me a story from Disneyland's first year of operation, 1955. Nunis was in charge of training the people who operated the park's attractions, such as the Jungle Cruise. One day when Nunis was on duty, Walt showed up at the Jungle Cruise and took a ride on the attraction. Nunis waited nervously until Walt returned, and he could tell at a glance that the boss was not happy. Stepping onto the dock, Walt said, "Dick, how long is the cruise supposed to take?"

"Seven minutes, Walt."

"Well, that trip took just over four minutes. Everything went by so fast that I couldn't tell the elephants from the hippos! I want you to retrain the boat operators."

So Nunis spent the next week working individually with each operator, timing each one with a stopwatch. When Walt made his next surprise inspection, he rode with every operator of every boat—and each cruise lasted exactly seven minutes.

"Walt was happy," Nunis told me. "He demanded excellence from every member of the organization, and he got it. No detail ever escaped his notice."

Thirty years after I had that conversation with Nunis, the Disney family invited me to attend the grand opening of the Walt Disney Family Museum in San Francisco. I was struck by a quotation that was displayed at the museum. I thought of Walt timing his Jungle Cruise operators when I read:

"We can lick them all with quality."—Walt Disney

* ★ *

Larry Catuzzi

A Leader Takes Bold Stands

Larry Catuzzi coached college football for many years, including four years as an assistant to Woody Hayes at Ohio State. Catuzzi was a quarterback at the University of Delaware when I was in high school in Wilmington, and we were teammates one summer on a semipro baseball team.

In 1999, my wife, Ruth, and I had dinner with Catuzzi. We talked about many fascinating subjects that evening, including the subject of leadership. As Catuzzi talked, I took out a pen and jotted down some of his words on a napkin. He said, "The one character trait all the great leaders have is toughness—mental and physical toughness, the ability to deal with hard situations and difficult people. A real leader takes bold stands. You can't intimidate him, and he doesn't hesitate to wade into tough situations and confront people when necessary."

Having known Catuzzi for most of my life, I can say that he exemplifies the very qualities he described. He is toughness personified.[2]

★ ★ ★

Bill Gaither

Envisioning the Future

Gospel singer Bill Gaither is the Babe Ruth of Christian music. He and his wife, Gloria, have composed more than seven hundred songs, including such favorites as "He Touched Me," "Because He Lives," and the anthem of triumph, "The King Is Coming." Gaither is a great basketball fan, and he loves to talk hoops.

In December 1985, while I was still the general manager of the Philadelphia 76ers, I was thinking seriously about building an NBA expansion team from the ground up. I visited Orlando, but I came back from Florida questioning whether that community could support an NBA franchise. The day after my Orlando trip, I went into my office in Philadelphia and the phone rang. It was Bill Gaither, and he wanted to talk basketball.

We chatted for a while, then out of the clear blue sky he said, "You know, Pat, what I really want to do is what you're doing. I want to run an NBA team."

"Oh? Do you know any teams that have an interest for sale?"

"No, no, not an existing team. I'd want to run an *expansion* team."

Well, that came as a bit of a shock. I wondered if he had been reading my mail! So I said, "An expansion team? Where would you put this new team?"

"Only one place to be. Orlando, Florida."

Wow! He *had* to be reading my mail! Not wanting to let on that I had just visited that very city, I said, "Why Orlando of all places?"

"We've played a lot of concert dates there, Pat," he said, "and there's something about Orlando that's different from other cities. There's a unique spirit there. It's a family place. I keep thinking it would be a nice place to retire to, and if I could own a piece of an NBA team in Orlando, it would complete the dream."

I had been having second thoughts about Orlando, but that conversation with Gaither tipped me back in its direction. As things turned out, Gaither never did buy a piece of the team, but he shared his dream with me, and that added a little oomph to my own expansion dream. From then on, I pursued a franchise in Orlando for all it was worth, and the rest is history.

The first task of leadership is vision. Bill Gaither is a man of vision, and he helped confirm my vision of a new NBA franchise in Orlando, Florida.

★ ★ ★

Michael Eisner and Frank Wells

"Every Walt Needs a Roy"

In September 1986, I received an invitation to a huge event at Epcot celebrating the fifteenth anniversary of Walt Disney World. The list of invited guests included VIPs from various fields of endeavor: business, entertainment, and sports. I bumped into Buell Duncan, the chairman of SunBank, and we chatted for a while about our efforts to bring NBA basketball to Orlando.

"The guy you need to talk to," Buell said, "is Michael Eisner." At that time, Eisner had been the CEO of the Walt Disney Company for about two years.

"Buell," I said, "I'd love to meet Michael Eisner. Can you arrange it?"

"Sure," he said. "I'll introduce you."

So Buell took me over to the American Pavilion in Epcot, where Eisner was on a platform flanked by Senator Ted Kennedy and Supreme Court Justice Warren Burger.

"Buell," I said, "Eisner looks kinda busy."

"Just wait here," Buell said. "He'll want to talk to you." And Buell turned and walked away. I was on my own.

Never one to be shy, I waded into the crowd as Eisner finished his remarks. In person, I found him to be taller, more imposing, and more impressive than he appeared on television. When I got close enough to make eye contact with him, I extended my hand and said, "Mr. Eisner, I'm—"

"Pat Williams!" Eisner said, pumping my hand. "You're just the man I want to talk to!"

"I am?" I said, stunned.

"Absolutely. We need to talk."

"We do? When?"

"Now," Eisner said. "Tonight. It's eight o'clock now. Let's meet in Paris at nine."

Eisner's assistant stepped forward and said, "You have an appointment with Chief Justice Burger at nine, Mr. Eisner."

"You tell Burger he's going to have to wait for me," Eisner said curtly.

For a moment, I wondered how Eisner and I were going to get to Paris by nine. Even if the Concorde could make the trip in an hour, it doesn't fly out of Orlando. Then it hit me: "Paris" is Disneyese for the French Pavilion at Epcot.

An hour later, I met Michael Eisner in "Paris," and we had a fascinating conversation, just the two of us. It turned out that he had been following our efforts with the NBA with great interest, and he wanted Disney to become a part-owner of the team. Though Disney didn't become a partner in our venture, the Magic continues to enjoy a mutually supportive relationship with Disney.

I see some distinct resemblances between Michael Eisner and Walt Disney. Eisner had been the studio chief at Paramount before he and Warner Brothers executive Frank Wells were brought in to run the Walt Disney Company. Like Walt, Eisner was a visionary at Disney—an idea man, an entrepreneur who could peer into the future and see possibilities. I met Frank Wells a few times, and I noticed that Eisner and Wells made a great team, much like the team of Walt Disney and his brother Roy Disney.

Walt and Roy were polar opposites. Walt was the idea man, the dreamer, while Roy was the accountant, the practical one. Michael Eisner was like Walt; Frank Wells was like Roy. It seems that so many successful partnerships are built on that kind of yin and yang relationship.

At Ben & Jerry's Ice Cream, Ben Cohen is the extrovert, the marketing genius, while Jerry Greenfield is the introvert, the one in charge of testing recipes and manufacturing the product. At Microsoft, Bill Gates was Walt, and Paul Allen was Roy. At Hewlett-Packard, William Hewlett was Walt, and David Packard was Roy. At Amway, Rich DeVos was Walt, and Jay Van Andel was Roy.

At Disney in the 1980s and early 1990s, Michael Eisner and Frank Wells had that same kind of relationship. Then, on Easter 1994, Wells was killed in a helicopter crash while returning from a ski trip in Nevada. His death, I think, was the beginning of the end for Eisner at Disney. Eisner was never the same after Wells was gone, and he stepped down in early 2005.

As my friend (and Disney expert) Peggy Matthews Rose once observed, "Every Walt needs a Roy, and every Roy needs a Walt."

★ ★ ★

Watson Spoelstra

"We Toss the Coin, But . . ."

In the summer of 1988, our dream of planting an NBA expansion team in central Florida was finally becoming a reality. We received our expansion lists from the other NBA teams—lists of players we could draft from the teams in order to build our roster—and began to zero in on the players we wanted.

We would also get to enter the college draft. In a halftime ceremony during the Lakers-Pistons finals, a coin flip would decide whether the Orlando Magic or the Minnesota Timberwolves would get to go first in the expansion draft. Our head coach, Matt Guokas, would be in LA to call the toss.

Events like high-stakes coin tosses usually make a nervous wreck out of me. But on the morning of the big expansion coin toss, my friend Watson Spoelstra called me. Spoelstra (who passed away in 1999) was then a retired Detroit sportswriter living in St. Petersburg. "Pat," he said, "I know how nervous you get when there's a lot riding on a coin toss. But I'd like you to look up Proverbs 16:33 in *The Living Bible*. I think the message in that verse is meant just for you, and I think it will help you survive the suspense of this day."

I thanked him, then looked up the verse. In it, a wise old man named Solomon observed, "We toss the coin, but it is the Lord who controls its decision" (TLB). That was exactly what I needed to hear, and I didn't feel a twinge of nervousness after reading that verse.

That evening, our conference room was filled with sports reporters and Magic executives listening in on a telephone hookup between LA and Orlando. Out in Los Angeles, Commissioner David Stern flipped the coin.

Matt Guokas called it.

The future of our organization glittered in the air.

The coin bounced on the carpet—and came up Magic.

We went into our very first expansion draft with the number one pick.

★ ★ ★

George McGovern

"I'd Rather Live the Adventure"

In October 1996, I went to Washington, DC, for the twenty-seventh running of the Marine Corps Marathon. Before the race, I chatted with the woman next to me. She told me she came from Baltimore and was running her first marathon. The slogan on her T-shirt read, "When Was the Last Time You Did Something for the First Time?"

I said, "I love that attitude!"

Minutes later, the race began. After three or four miles, I noticed a gray-haired woman who was keeping an easy pace. I moved up beside her and said, "How are you doing?"

"Fine, just fine," she said—and she was. This grandmotherly woman wasn't even breathing hard.

"I'm from Orlando," I said. "Where are you from?"

"College Park, Maryland," she said, "and I know what you're wondering, so I might as well tell you. I'm eighty-two, and this is my eighth marathon. I ran my first marathon when I was seventy-three."

I could only imagine the conversation between this woman and her kids and grandkids. "Grandma, are you crazy? A marathon? At your age? What if you fall and break your hip?" But I had seen the joy on her face. I don't know if her kids and grandkids understood why she was running that marathon, but I understood. I had that same look of joy on my face when I crossed the finish line.

I had taken on a challenge, and I had finished my course. Along the way, I had met two women who lived boldly and demonstrated the attitude of a winner. But the day was not over. That evening, I would meet another kind of marathon runner, and I would be inspired once more.

The "runner" I met over dinner that evening was former senator George McGovern of South Dakota. The "marathon" he ran was the race for the presidency. He ran against Richard Nixon in 1972 and lost in a landslide, but McGovern is still a winner in my book. As we talked, he showed me the attitude of a champion.

McGovern was a decorated bomber pilot in World War II.

He risked death every time he climbed into the cockpit of a B-24 Liberator. On his thirty-fifth mission over Europe—which was scheduled to be his final bombing run before returning Stateside—he flew through a hailstorm of flak. The antiaircraft fire shredded the plane's hydraulics, punched more than a hundred holes in the fuselage, and left his waist gunner critically wounded. McGovern had to invent a landing technique that was not in the training manual, but he brought his crew back alive, including the waist gunner.

As we talked, McGovern shared stories about his political battles, his famous friends (including John F. Kennedy), and his opponents, especially Richard Nixon. He even told me about a young go-getter who was his campaign director for the state of Texas in 1972—a fella from Arkansas named Bill Clinton. McGovern suffered one of the worst defeats in the annals of presidential politics, carrying only Massachusetts and the District of Columbia. He even lost his home state of South Dakota.

I asked, "How did it feel to lose so badly?"

"I knew it was an uphill fight from the beginning," he said. "To start with, I had to defeat an unprecedented field of seventeen candidates to win the Democratic nomination. Then I had to go up against a popular sitting president. People who only remember Nixon because of Watergate forget that he had high approval ratings in 1972. Sure, it hurt losing in such a big landslide, but I have no regrets. It was the chance of a lifetime, and I went for it. Remember Marv Levy? He coached the Buffalo Bills to four consecutive Super Bowls and lost all four. He said, 'I'd rather get to this final level and lose than be sitting home watching.' That's the way I look at it. I'd rather live the adventure than be a spectator to world events."

McGovern didn't reach the White House, but he lived the

adventure. He lost the election, but he maintained the attitude of a winner.

★ ★ ★

Buck O'Neil and Ernie Banks

"Courage Is Part of Living"

They call Ernie Banks "Mr. Cub" and "Mr. Sunshine." For nineteen seasons, from 1953 to 1971, Banks played shortstop and first baseman for the Chicago Cubs. Before that, he played for the Kansas City Monarchs of the Negro League.

I was the general manager of the Bulls from 1969 to 1973, and during my time in Chicago, Banks was an icon, a saint, a beloved hero in the "City of the Big Shoulders." Banks was a big basketball fan, and he often came to Bulls games. If we ever wanted to get the crowd going, all we had to do was introduce Banks. He'd take a bow while fifteen thousand people would stamp, hoot, and holler.

One day, Banks was in Orlando helping out with the central Florida farm club that the Cubs had at that time. I went to his hotel and interviewed him for my radio show. As we chatted, I mentioned the fact that he was famous for always being upbeat and cheerful. No matter how the Cubs were struggling—and they were *always* struggling—his catchphrase was, "Let's play two today!" In other words, let's play two games today—it's too great a day for just one.

86

"Ernie," I said, "what makes you so optimistic? How did you develop that outlook on life?"

"The key person in my life," Ernie said, "was Buck O'Neil. He was a coach with the Kansas City Monarchs, so I knew him from the Negro League. I was around Buck a lot, and he always stressed the importance of a positive outlook, an optimistic approach to life. He said, 'You can be downtrodden and pessimistic and mad at the world, but what does that get you?' Buck wouldn't allow that. I saw what optimism did in his life and the kind of uplifting impact he had on everyone he met. I thought, 'That's the way to do it.' That's how I've been doing it my whole career, just like Buck taught me."

Buck O'Neil had worked as a scout for the Chicago Cubs and the Kansas City Royals, and I had sat behind home plate with him at spring training games in Orlando. He had a charismatic influence, and the fans (including me) flocked to him for the chance to talk baseball with him. O'Neil was exactly as Banks described him: optimistic, forward looking, full of the joy of living. No wonder Banks was the way he was. His life had been influenced and impacted by Buck O'Neil.

O'Neil passed away in 2006 at the age of ninety-four. I had the rare privilege of interviewing him just a few months before his death. Raised under segregation in Florida, he was working in the fields packing celery when he was twelve. He decided he didn't want to do backbreaking field labor for the rest of his life, and after attending a semipro baseball game in West Palm Beach, he knew he wanted to be a ballplayer.

Though segregation at first kept him from playing in the major leagues, O'Neil never surrendered to bitterness. "My generation did the groundwork for the guys who play the game today," he told me. "I don't want anyone feeling sorry for me. Every generation has its part to play. We all have our duty."

O'Neil's sense of duty served him well as a ballplayer. During two decades in the Negro League, he posted a .288 career batting average (including a career-best .358 in 1947). In 2006, he was nominated for admission into the Baseball Hall of Fame, but he failed to receive enough votes for induction. Though the sports world was shocked at O'Neil's rejection, he was upbeat. "God's been good to me," he told a crowd of disappointed fans. "They didn't think Buck was good enough to be in the Hall of Fame. That's the way they thought about it and that's the way it is, so we're going to live with that. Now, if I'm a Hall of Famer for you, that's all right with me. Just keep loving old Buck. Don't weep for Buck. No, man, be happy, be thankful."

As O'Neil told me in our interview, "In the Negro League, you had to hang in there. There were so many good ballplayers who wanted to take your job away. Courage is part of living. There's always going to be obstacles and troubles out there. You've got to have the courage to stay in there."

No wonder Buck O'Neil's attitude had such an impact on Ernie Banks—and, yes, on Pat Williams. He had the attitude of a winner and a positive role model. And that's the attitude of a leader.

★ ★ ★

Moses Malone

"It's Never Easy for Moses"

I was the general manager of the Philadelphia 76ers in 1983, when we made our championship run. Our center was Moses Malone, who enjoyed a twenty-one-year NBA career and a spot on the NBA's all-time top 50 team. Malone was a tireless athlete, a dependable scorer, and one of the greatest offensive rebounders in the game.

Malone should not have been one of the greatest players in NBA history, yet he clearly was. At six ten, he was big but certainly not the tallest center in the game. There were a lot of players in the NBA with greater height, larger hands, faster legs, a higher vertical leap, and a more accurate shot, yet Malone somehow managed to be the best in the game.

After many hours watching him play, I could think of only one explanation for his greatness: Moses Malone had the attitude of a winner. He believed. He competed hard. He thrived on intense physical competition. The rougher it got, the better he played. The more hands an opponent put up in his face, the more accurate his shot. The longer the game went, the stronger he became. And he never quit. Malone may well have been the hardest-working player in the history of the game. He had an interesting habit of talking about himself in the third person, and he explained himself this way: "It's never easy for Moses. Moses got to get out there every night and work hard."

In many ways, Malone appeared to be a mismatch for the 76ers' high-velocity style. Coach Billy Cunningham had been trying to ratchet up the team's speed and quickness—and then we added Malone, a center with a slow-down style. There was no way to know what the team chemistry would be like until all the team ingredients—Malone, Dr. J, Andrew Toney, Maurice Cheeks, Bobby Jones, and the rest—were put together out on the court.

But Malone had something going for him that nobody counted on: the attitude of a winner. He wasn't interested in personal glory. He just wanted his team to do well. In a quiet, self-effacing way, Malone stood before reporters in Philadelphia and humbly said, "This team is Doc's show. I've got a chance to play with Doc, and I think it's gonna be a better show. I'm just gonna play my game—attack the boards, go to the offensive boards, look for the fast break, look to rebound."

In his first season with the 76ers, Moses led our team to the Promised Land—an NBA championship. During the victory parade down Philadelphia's Broad Street, our players were feted with cheers and confetti, and Moses Malone received a special honor. As his vehicle passed a construction site, about twenty construction workers picked up their lunch pails and held them out toward Malone. Those working-class lunch pails were a fitting tribute to the hardworking player who helped bring a championship to Philly.

One of the paradoxes of authentic leadership is that a true leader is a servant of those he leads. Moses Malone saw himself as a servant of his teammates—and his serving heart was the key to his greatness as a leader.

★ ★ ★

Chuck Daly

"We Want to Be Happy after the Games"

Rollie Massimino coaches men's basketball at Northwood University in West Palm Beach, Florida. He earned his coaching chops as an assistant to Chuck Daly at the University of Pennsylvania in the 1970s. When Massimino was hired to coach at Northwood in 2006, Daly was his biggest booster and attended every home game.

In 2009, when Daly was hospitalized for pancreatic cancer, Massimino went to visit him every day. Though Daly grew weaker by the day, he always had enough strength to needle his former assistant. "Rollie," he'd say, "have you signed any good players? Remember, we want to be happy after the games."

Massimino knew what Daly meant. The way to be happy after a game is to win. And to win, you've got to have a talented, well-balanced team—a team with good chemistry and no bad apples. Even in the closing days of his life, Daly was mentoring Massimino and helping to sharpen his coaching skills.

★ ★ ★

NBA Coaches

"Will He Listen?"

I've been an NBA executive since 1968, and I have been privileged to work alongside some of the legendary coaches of the game: Chuck Daly, Matt Guokas, Jack Ramsay, Dick Motta, Cotton Fitzsimmons, Gene Shue, Billy Cunningham, Brian Hill, Doc Rivers, Stan Van Gundy, and many more. Each of these coaches approaches the game in his own unique way. Yet, at one time or another, I've heard all of them ask the same essential question when scouting and recruiting new players: "Can I coach him? Will he listen to me? Does he have a teachable spirit?"

If coachability and teachability are so important in the NBA, at the highest level of the game, then these qualities are certainly important at every other level, and in every leadership arena. When you are assembling a team or an organization, the people you recruit must be eager to listen and to learn.

★ ★ ★

Rudy Giuliani

Four Leadership Principles

After Rudy Giuliani spoke at a seminar at our arena, he invited me into his private room for a chat. He could not have been more gracious. I came prepared to learn, so I opened my notebook and, with my pen poised over the page, said, "Mayor Giuliani, what does it take to be a great leader?"

"In my experience," he said, "there are four essential principles for being a great leader. If you do all four, and do them well, you can't miss.

"First, set realistic goals for your team. People work better if they have goals to shoot for. The goals should be challenging but achievable.

"Second, be a teacher. A leader should challenge his or her people to continually learn, grow, and improve. You have to practice important skills over and over until people master the fundamentals. Keep teaching, keep practicing, keep correcting, keep instructing. That's how you cut down on the number of mistakes.

"Third, build the confidence of your people. Believe in them and stick with them through the tough times. Set high standards but be patient with them as they strive to attain those standards.

"Fourth, encourage your people to relax, to conquer fear, and to overcome worry. Nothing kills a performance like performance anxiety. Golf is a great example. You have to stay loose. You have to be relaxed in order to perform well. If you're anxious about your backswing or afraid of making a mistake, you'll blow it. The more relaxed you are, the better you perform."

That's great leadership advice from the man called "America's Mayor."

★ ★ ★

Howard Schultz

"We're Not in the Coffee Business"

A number of years ago, I had a fascinating conversation with Howard Schultz, the man who bought a three-coffeehouse chain in 1987 and expanded it into the Starbucks empire. Today, there are almost twenty-one thousand Starbucks coffeehouses in sixty-two countries around the world.

"In a company of that size," I said, "where do leaders come from?"

"Our leaders come from within our ranks," he said. "We're opening three stores a day, and we've got to promote from within. You can't run a Starbucks store unless you're steeped in the Starbucks culture."

"So how do you spot leadership talent? How do you know when someone is ready to lead?"

"People skills," he said. "Customer satisfaction is the key to the growth of our company. In order to be a leader at Starbucks, you've got to have outstanding people skills. We're not in the coffee business. We're in the people business. That's what Starbucks is all about."

★ ★ ★

Red Auerbach

"He Listened"

When I became the general manager of the Chicago Bulls in the fall of 1969, I was twenty-nine years old and doing business with some longtime veterans of the NBA wars, including Red Auerbach, who was then the general manager of the Celtics. Talk about intimidating! I'd go to league meetings and there would be the legendary Red Auerbach chomping on a cigar, wearing all his championship rings. To him, I was a wet-behind-the-ears kid from Chicago.

As the years went on, Auerbach became a great friend. He was always available to me and freely gave me sage advice when I needed it. He was a wise and generous mentor to me and many others.

After Auerbach's death in 2006, I had Tom Heinsohn as a guest on my radio show. Heinsohn was a longtime Celtics player, coach, and broadcaster who played for Auerbach in the glory years. I said to him, "Tell me about Red Auerbach. What did he do that set him apart as a leader?"

"He listened to his players," Heinsohn said, "and that made us all believe it was our team. He immersed us in everything that was going on. For example, Red might come up with a new play in the summer, and he'd lay it out for us and teach it to us in training camp in the fall. Then he'd say, 'What do you guys think?' We all got a chance to share our feelings and insights. Because he asked for our input, we all had a proprietary interest in the outcome of each practice and game.

"Here's another example of the way Red listened. We'd be

95

in the huddle with two minutes to go and trailing by ten points. Red would say, 'Does anybody have something here?' Different guys would offer their ideas, then Red would make a decision based on what his players thought. And because the players had made a commitment in front of their teammates, they were locked in. When players buy in and take ownership, their motivation and intensity go way up. That's why it's important for coaches to listen. Red Auerbach listened, and that's why he was a great leader."

★ ★ ★

Chuck Daly

A Suffering Business

In 1977, we hired Chuck Daly as an assistant coach to Billy Cunningham for the Philadelphia 76ers. Daly became a good friend, and we later hired him as head coach of the Orlando Magic—at a much steeper salary. He often needled me about the paltry sum we paid him in 1977, but I would reply, "Chuck, we got you cheap, but you certainly made up for it later."

Daly had a wonderful way of expressing wise life principles. In the 1998–99 season, Daly coached the Magic into the playoffs, and we were eliminated by Washington in a very tough series. The next morning, Daly came into my office and sat down by my desk. "Ours is a suffering business," he said with a sigh.

"Chuck," I said, "tell me what you mean."

"Everybody goes home suffering. The teams that don't get into the play-offs are suffering. Of the teams that *do* get into the play-offs, most get knocked out and their dreams of a championship are dashed, so they are suffering even worse. Eventually, you get down to the two teams in the finals, and only one of those two teams will be victorious. The other team will go home as the loser. They will be suffering most of all because they came so close only to have their hopes dashed. Of all the teams that begin the season, only one team goes home happy. Ours is a suffering business."

Daly had another great expression that he used from time to time: Never trust happiness. In other words, you might have won three or four games in a row, you might have everybody playing well, feeling motivated, and happy, and it could all go away with one bad game. So Daly would warn his players, "Never trust happiness." Never get complacent. Always stay hungry, stay focused, because happiness can vanish in a hurry.

Daly also had a midnight rule. When the game is over, you've got until midnight to celebrate or to drown your sorrows, but promptly at 12:01, you must start focusing on winning the next game.

When Daly passed away in the spring of 2009, it was a sad day for all of us who knew and loved him. He was a leader who injected a lot of fun into this "suffering business," and I miss him to this day.

★ ★ ★

Kevin Durant

"Be Praying for Pat Williams"

Kevin Durant is a star forward for the Oklahoma City Thunder, and he has been the anchor of that franchise for a number of years. Back when the team was not a good team yet, and they were getting some high draft picks, Durant would go to the draft and greet the new players after his team had drafted them. That was unheard-of.

After the draft, he would immediately come to Orlando for our summer league, which is for draft picks and free agents. He'd spend the whole week scrimmaging and working with the young Thunder players, demonstrating a difference-making level of involvement and leadership.

In January 2011, I announced that I had been diagnosed with multiple myeloma. Durant went straight to his Twitter account and tweeted out the message "Be praying for Pat Williams of the Magic."

Durant and I didn't really know each other, yet he saw the news and wanted people to pray for me. That really meant a lot to me. Durant has a strong faith and a strong character. He's a leader on the court and a spiritual leader among his teammates.

★ ★ ★

Michael S. Dukakis

Leadership Is Service to Others

Michael S. Dukakis was elected governor of Massachusetts in 1974, inheriting a massive deficit and record high unemployment. Under his leadership, Massachusetts emerged from one of the worst economic disasters in state history. Dukakis was elected again in 1982 and 1986 by wide margins. He won the Democratic nomination for president in 1988 but lost the presidential race to George H. W. Bush.

I once asked Governor Dukakis how he became interested in politics and leadership. "I ran for third grade class president at the age of eight," he said. "I just wanted to exercise leadership, even at that very young age. As I grew older, I received encouragement from my teachers.

"I grew up in a community where there were many opportunities for political leadership. Brookline, just outside of Boston, is a town of about fifty-five thousand people—big enough, but not so big that you had to raise a fortune just to run for local office. The volunteers who helped me in my campaigns were absolutely crucial to my success.

"I'm concerned these days about our ability to attract young leaders for public service. I'm concerned about a climate in our country that often paints the worst picture of public service.

"There's nothing quite so personally fulfilling as being in a position where you can have a real impact on the lives of your fellow citizens, and that is what political leadership—political service—gives someone a chance to do."

★ ★ ★

Doc Rivers

"Are You Committed?"

Glenn "Doc" Rivers is currently the head coach of the Los Angeles Clippers. Before that, he served as head coach of the Orlando Magic (1999–2003) and the Boston Celtics (2004–13). As coach of the Magic, Doc got to work alongside his hero, Julius Erving. In fact, Doc got his nickname from NCAA coach Rick Majerus after young Rivers showed up at basketball camp wearing a "Dr. J" T-shirt.

When Doc took over in Orlando, the team was still reeling from the dismantling of a stellar lineup that had included Shaquille O'Neal, Penny Hardaway, Horace Grant, and Nick Anderson. He faced some tough challenges in rebuilding the team.

Doc went to great lengths to get his message across to his players. On one occasion, he wanted to make sure his leading scorer, point guard Darrell Armstrong, was fully committed to the goal of a successful season, so he sent him a message via Federal Express. When Armstrong ripped open the envelope, he found a single sheet of paper with three words typed in the center: "Are You Committed?"

Doc lived only fifteen minutes from Armstrong's house. He could have driven that sheet of paper over and placed it in Armstrong's hand for far less trouble and expense than it took to send it. But Doc wanted to make sure Armstrong got the message. And he did.

During his time in Orlando, Doc continually preached his four respect rules to the team. Respect your teammates. Respect your coaches. Respect yourself. Respect your family's name.

Those are rules to live by. If you respect your teammates, you'll build unity on the team. If you respect your coaches, you'll build harmony throughout the team. If you respect yourself, you'll have dignity wherever you go. And if you respect your family's name, you'll build a reputation to be proud of.

★ ★ ★

Cal Ripken Jr.

The Ink-Stained Hand

One time, when the Ted Williams Museum and Hitters Hall of Fame was still in Hernando, north of Orlando, Cal Ripken Jr. was there. He and many other great ballplayers were signing autographs. I noticed that the line at Ripken's table looked the longest and hardly moved at all. Looking closer, I realized why.

At many of the other tables, the ballplayers had an assembly line going, but Ripken spent four or five minutes with each person who came for an autograph, asking who they were and where they were from, answering their questions about his career, giving them a word of motivation and inspiration.

As I watched him sign, I noticed that his left hand was marked up with ink. Before he'd write his autograph, he'd take his pen and wipe the point on his left hand so that the ink wouldn't blob up and smear when he signed. Then he'd look up and thank the fan and chat for a bit. The line moved at a snail's pace because Ripken took the time to engage with every fan.

He recently came to our arena before a Magic game to sign copies of *Squeeze Play*, his latest baseball novel for young readers. Just as he had at the Ted Williams Museum event, he chatted with each fan, got his photo taken with them—and blotted the excess ink on his hand before he inscribed each book. Cal Ripken Jr. is more than a Hall of Fame baseball player—he's a Hall of Fame human being.

Leaders are role models, and Cal Ripken Jr. is an example to all his fans of what it means to be a leader—and a servant.

★ ★ ★

Larry O'Brien

The Wrath of the Commissioner

Larry O'Brien was a key strategist of John F. Kennedy's presidential campaign in 1960 and served as the postmaster general under Lyndon B. Johnson. He was appointed commissioner of the NBA in 1975, and his appointment helped to raise the stature and prominence of professional basketball.

An Irish-American from Massachusetts, he was an elegant, bespectacled man with a precise, businesslike way of speaking. When you met him and talked to him, you felt you were in the presence of royalty. But if you crossed him—look out!

Early in the 1979–80 season, our Philadelphia 76ers played in Kansas City. Our powerful young center Darryl Dawkins went up for a dunk from the right side. The only Kansas City defender under the hoop was Bill Robinzine. Seeing that the dunk was a done deal, Robinzine made no move to block the shot. Dawkins smashed the rim with such force that the backboard exploded, showering him and Robinzine with thousands of pieces of glass.

The exploding backboard was an awesome sight—something that had never been seen before in the NBA. The officials halted the game for about forty-five minutes to mop up the floor and replace the backboard.

Dawkins became an instant celebrity, and he used his formidable gift of gab to maximize his fame. He dubbed himself "The Dawk," "Chocolate Thunder," and "The Master of Disaster."

The dunk was replayed again and again on television sports shows, but the NBA brass was not amused. In a chilly phone call from New York, Larry O'Brien informed me in no uncertain terms, "That is not to happen again."

I said, "I understand, sir."

Three weeks later, it happened again.

We hosted the San Antonio Spurs at the Spectrum. Once more, Dawkins went up for a dunk and came back to earth in a meteor shower of broken glass.

In the excitement of the moment, I forgot Commissioner O'Brien's warning. All I could see at that moment were the vast promotional possibilities. I ran out onto the floor with a paper bag and scooped up all the glass I could. Later, we announced that we would give away souvenir pieces of busted backboard glass at our next home game.

The next morning, I received another phone call from the NBA office in New York summoning Dawkins and me to the commissioner's office. So we took a bus from South Jersey to the terminal in New York. We walked up Fifth Avenue, and people along the way pointed, waved, and shouted, "Hey, Chocolate Thunder!" Dawkins enjoyed all the attention, but it only made me more miserable. I was not looking forward to facing Commissioner O'Brien.

We arrived at the NBA office, and a receptionist ushered us into the solemn, morgue-quiet office of the commissioner. O'Brien eyed us coldly. Dawkins and I meekly took our seats.

"I thought we had an agreement," O'Brien said, "that this was never to happen again." He pointed out that many arenas weren't equipped with extra backboards, so this wanton destruction of backboards simply could not be allowed.

For his part, Dawkins was very contrite. The shattered backboards, he said, were "accidents."

O'Brien leaned forward. "There will be no more 'accidents,' Mr. Dawkins. Is that clear?"

"Yes, sir. It won't happen again, sir."

Receiving that assurance, O'Brien visibly relaxed, and the atmosphere became a little less chilly. So I said, "You know, we gathered up all those pieces of glass and we're going to give them away as souvenirs next weekend. We're calling it Darryl Dawkins Shatterday Night!"

As soon as the words were out of my mouth, I knew I'd made a huge mistake. O'Brien's jaw dropped, and a vein throbbed at his temple. He came halfway out of his chair and extended a threatening forefinger. "There will be no promotion and no souvenir glass. Do you understand?"

"Absolutely, sir," I said. "It will never be mentioned again."

The result of those incidents was a new league rule—the "Dawkins Rule." Any player who shattered a backboard would be automatically ejected, fined, and made ineligible to play the following game. The shatterings also led to the use of snap-back rims that reduced the stress on backboards.

I learned a lot that day from O'Brien about the importance of firm, decisive leadership. In time, he became a good friend, and I often enjoyed our chats about his service in Washington under JFK and LBJ.

But I never again risked the wrath of the commissioner.

$$\star \; \bigstar \; \star$$

Pat Riley

"Don't Be Afraid to Coach the Team"

In 1981, Pat Riley decided to leave the broadcast booth and become the head coach of the Los Angeles Lakers. Though he'd had a successful playing career, he had no coaching experience, not even as an assistant. Yet there he was, preparing to coach a team made up of highly talented, strong-willed, temperamental athletes. This was the era of Kareem Abdul-Jabbar and Magic Johnson, so it would take a strong leader to coach that bunch. In fact, it didn't take long before his players began to challenge his authority and test his will. As a result, Riley began to doubt himself.

After one practice, Lakers majority owner Jerry Buss took him aside and said, "Pat, a word of advice. Don't be afraid to coach the team." That's all Buss said, but Riley got the message. As he later told me, "That's the single best piece of leadership advice I've ever gotten."

★ ★ ★
Fitz Dixon

"Go Get It Done"

When I was the general manager of the Philadelphia 76ers, I heard that Julius Erving—the legendary Dr. J—was unhappy with his team, the New York Nets, and was going to sit out training camp in the fall of 1976. So I called the Nets' general manager, Bill Melchionni, and told him we wanted to acquire Erving. Melchionni told me it would cost six million dollars—three million to the Nets and three million to Erving.

I swallowed hard, then went to talk to our team's new owner, Fitz Dixon. He had just purchased the 76ers for eight million dollars, and I was about to ask him to spend three-quarters of that amount on just one player! I was sure he'd never go for it, but I had to try.

I found our owner sitting at his desk.

"Mr. Dixon," I said, "we have an opportunity to get a really special player on our team. His name is—" I paused for dramatic effect, "Julius Erving."

I thought Mr. Dixon would jump up with excitement. Instead, he looked befuddled. "Who?"

I could hardly believe it. The owner of the Philadelphia 76ers had never even heard of Dr. J!

Then I remembered that Dixon was fairly new to the sports world. He was an educator, a philanthropist, a Harvard man, the son of a wealthy banker, the husband of an heiress. He had become a basketball fan just a few weeks before purchasing the team. He really had no clue who Erving was. How could I explain Dr. J to Dixon in a single sentence?

I said, "Julius Erving is the Babe Ruth of basketball."

Dixon's eyes lit up. We understood each other.

"How much will it cost me to acquire Mr. Erving's talents?"

I gulped hard. "Six million dollars, sir."

He didn't even flinch. "Are you recommending the deal?"

I gulped again. "Yes, sir," I said firmly, "I am."

Dixon nodded slowly. Then he smiled at me and said, "Well, go get it done." Then he added one of his favorite expressions: "That'll be just fine and dandy."

I could hardly believe what had just happened. In a matter of seconds, on the strength of my recommendation alone, Dixon had just made a six-million-dollar decision.

And he never regretted it.

★ ★ ★

Mike Krzyzewski

"No Excuse, Sir"

As a lowly plebe at the Point in 1965, Duke head basketball coach Mike Krzyzewski discovered a tradition the cadets called "Beast Barracks." For two months, upperclassmen treat plebes as the lowest form of life. When an upperclassman asks a question, the miserable plebe is allowed only one of three possible answers: "Yes, sir," "No, sir," or "No excuse, sir."

During "Beast Barracks," Cadet Krzyzewski was walking on the campus with his roommate. Both cadets were in full uniform. The roommate stepped in a puddle, splashing mud on Krzyzewski's shoes. Moments later, Krzyzewski saw two upperclassmen approaching. "Halt!" said one.

Krzyzewski came to a full stop. The upperclassmen looked the two plebes up and down. They told Krzyzewski's roommate he was free to go, but Krzyzewski had to stand at attention. "Your shoes are all cruddy," one upperclassman said. "Why?"

Krzyzewski wanted to blame his roommate for splashing mud on his shoes, but excuses were not allowed, so he replied, "No excuse, sir."

The upperclassman screamed insults at him, then wrote him up, giving him demerits for his dirty shoes.

At first, Krzyzewski was furious with his roommate because of the mud, but then he realized he really did have no excuse. He should have gone back to his room and changed his shoes. He learned a lesson in responsibility, and he concluded that there really are only three answers to any leadership question: "Yes, sir," "No, sir," and "No excuse, sir."

★ ★ ★

Harry S. Truman

"The Decision Was Mine"

In the early 1990s, Colonel Paul W. Tibbets Jr. was a guest on my radio show. Colonel Tibbets flew the atomic bomb mission over Hiroshima in 1945. It was fascinating—and sobering—to hear him describe the bombing mission that ended World War II. "When the bomb went off," he said, "I felt a tingling in the fillings of my teeth. I looked out and saw the mushroom cloud rising, and I knew that the city underneath that cloud had disappeared."

I asked Tibbets what he thought about as he flew back to Tinian Island.

"I was relieved," he said. "I knew the bomb would end the war and stop the killing. When Japan saw the effects of that bomb, they'd have to surrender. They had no choice. There was no doubt in my mind that millions of Americans and Japanese would have a chance to live out their lives because of what my crew and I had done that day."

I asked, "Did you ever meet Harry Truman?"

"Just once," he said. "After the war ended, President Truman invited me to the White House, and we had a conversation in the Oval Office. He thanked me for completing my mission, and then he said, 'Don't lose any sleep over it. You did what you had to do. The decision to send you was mine.'"

★ ★ ★

Donald Rumsfeld

An Integrity Check

Donald Rumsfeld served as the secretary of defense under two presidents, Gerald R. Ford (1975–77) and George W.

Bush (2001–6). In 2006, I signed a copy of my book *The Warrior Within* and mailed it to Rumsfeld in Washington, DC. A few days later, I received a note from him.

Dear Mr. Williams,

I received the signed copy of your book, The Warrior Within. *It was kind of you to think of me, and I appreciate it. Enclosed, please find my personal check to cover the appraised value as required by regulation. I would like to reimburse you for your nice gift.*

Sincerely,
Donald Rumsfeld

Included was a check made out to me for forty dollars, more than double the retail price of the book. I have sent books to government officials before, and that was the first time an official responded by sending a check for reimbursement. I was quite impressed, and I have Rumsfeld's letter and check framed on my wall.

★ ★ ★

Bobby Bowden

A Solid Foundation

Mark Richt, head football coach at the University of Georgia, told me how another legendary coach—Bobby Bowden, head football coach of the Florida State Seminoles from 1976 to 2009—exemplified integrity. "It was a life-changing experience," Richt said, "to serve as an assistant coach under a man of the caliber and character of Bobby Bowden.

"I was coming up the ranks as a college coach, and I'd heard a lot of war stories about how coaches need to break the rules and cut corners in order to put together a winning team. But soon after I took the job at Florida State, Coach Bowden eased my concerns. At one of the first coaches' meetings, he said, 'We will not do anything outside of the rules to recruit a player to our program. I will support everyone on this coaching staff in everything they do—except cheating to get recruits. This program is built on a foundation of integrity.'

"When I heard that, I knew I was in the right place. Coach Bowden always demanded integrity from his coaching staff, and he instilled integrity in all of his players."

★ ★ ★

Walter Winchell

Be Careful What You Say

Our era has largely forgotten Walter Winchell (1897–1972), but in the times I grew up in, he was the most well-known newspaper and radio gossip commentator in the country. From the late 1920s through the 1960s, fifty million people read his newspaper column every day. He made his radio debut on WABC in New York in 1930 and was the narrator of the television crime drama *The Untouchables* from 1959 to 1963. He was famed for his rapid-fire style of speaking; he could deliver his broadcasts at a rate of two hundred words per minute. For decades, there was hardly a person alive who couldn't instantly recognize the distinctive voice of Walter Winchell.

In 1967, I was the general manager of the Spartanburg Phillies. Our announcer was John Gordon. At the end of the season, Gordon and I decided to head to Fenway Park in Boston for the 1967 World Series between the Cardinals and the Red Sox. As we were hanging out among the legendary media personalities who were covering the game, Gordon spotted Winchell.

This was long before the era of cell phones, of course, but there was a pay phone nearby, so Gordon decided to call Jack Six, the host of the afternoon show on his radio station, WSPA in Spartanburg. He placed the call and got Jack Six on the line. "That's right, Jack!" Gordon said. "I'm at Fenway Park with Walter Winchell, and I want to put Winchell on the air with you."

Six said, "That's great! Put him on!"

Gordon turned to Winchell, handed him the phone, and said, "Walter, say hi to Jack Six!"

Unfortunately, Gordon neglected to tell Winchell that the phone call was going out live on the radio in Spartanburg. So Winchell grabbed the phone and said, "Who in the @#%& is Jack Six?"

The word Winchell used was the F bomb, unquestionably the most unairable word in the broadcast business. There was no delay button in those days, no safety net. The word went out live over the airwaves, turning the atmosphere blue over the entire city of Spartanburg.

Poor John Gordon! His mouth dropped open, his eyes bugged out, and his face turned as white as the paper his termination notice would be typed on. Gordon knew his broadcasting career was over. Yet he somehow managed to get through that debacle, and he became the radio voice of the Minnesota Twins for twenty-five years.

(I don't know what happened to Jack Six.)

The moral of the story: Be careful what you say. Especially in this era of smart phones and the internet, you never know when your words might be broadcast to the world.

★ ★ ★

Art Linkletter

Watch Your Intensifiers!

Art Linkletter was probably Walt Disney's closest friend. So, while I was writing a book about Walt, I had several conversations with Linkletter. During one of our chats, I said, "Walt was a very unique man, wasn't he?"

Linkletter stopped me right there. "The old schoolteacher is coming out in me," he said. "Forgive me for getting up on my soapbox, Pat, but a person either is or is not unique. There are no degrees of uniqueness. So you can't be somewhat unique or very unique or extremely unique. But you are absolutely right about Walt. He was unique. Simply unique."

Ever since Linkletter corrected me on my misuse of an intensifier, I've been aware of that mistake in my own speech and the speech of others. It's an amazingly common mistake, and now that I'm conscious of it, it really grates on me! Whenever I hear someone in the media refer to someone as "very unique," I feel like calling them up and saying, "The old schoolteacher in me feels compelled to point out—"

There's only one problem. Unlike Linkletter, I was never an old schoolteacher.

★ ★ ★

LeBron James

Poised and Articulate

LeBron James came out of high school highly celebrated and was drafted by the Cleveland Cavaliers. He made his debut in the Orlando summer league, a tournament for new draft picks and free agents. Normally, we hold the summer league in our practice gym, but having James there was such a big deal that we opened up the arena, and we almost packed the building.

After the summer league game, James conducted a press conference. The media room was packed, and I stood off to the side to take it all in. I was amazed to hear this eighteen-year-old youth, straight out of high school, handling the media like a pro. He answered their questions, remaining poised and in total control throughout.

He stayed focused on his message throughout the press conference, and that message was largely about his favorite cause—playgrounds for kids—and his corporate sponsor. He said, "Nike has agreed to sponsor playgrounds around the country, and I'm very grateful to them. Any more questions?" He took another question or two, then said, "That's all I have time for."

Then he was off the stage and out of view.

I thought, *How in the world does an eighteen-year-old develop the ability to be that poised, that articulate, that in control?* It's especially amazing when you realize he came from a deprived background with a teen mother and an out-of-the-picture father. Somewhere along the line—perhaps in high school or through the people who managed him professionally—he received some good instruction regarding public speaking and dealing with the media.

And he may have a natural communication ability to match his ball-handling skills.

★ ★ ★

Norman Schwarzkopf

"Talking to People Straight On"

Every year, the Magic organization stages a spring gala event to raise funds for the Magic Youth Foundation. One year, the guest of honor at the event was General Norman Schwarzkopf. The organizers asked me to be Schwarzkopf's host for the evening, and I was honored to spend time talking with the general.

I found "Stormin' Norman" Schwarzkopf to be very outgoing and friendly. I said, "General, do you ever think about the fact that a madman in Iraq, and his decision to take on the whole world and invade Kuwait, helped to make you a household name?"

"I think about it all the time," he said. "If it hadn't been for Sadaam Hussein, no one would have ever heard of me."

Schwarzkopf was frequently out on the speaking circuit, so I asked him, "What is the most important thing you've done to advance your speaking career?"

Without hesitation, he said, "I threw away my notes, came out from behind the lectern, and started just talking to people straight on."

His answer to my question had a big impact on me. During my speeches, I was still using note cards and standing behind a lectern. But Schwarzkopf rocked my world. I realized I needed to do what he did. So just like Stormin' Norman, I stopped using note cards and removed the barriers between my audience and me. And I love public speaking more than ever!

★ ★ ★

Joe Garagiola

The Three Speeches

Joe Garagiola is a former Major League Baseball catcher who later became a television personality, appearing on NBC's *Today* show for many years. I once asked him what he had learned during his career as a public speaker.

He told me, "I've learned four important lessons as a public speaker. First, you must believe in what you're saying—or nobody else will. Second, act as if you're among friends and you're there for a nice visit. Third, there's no such thing as an ad lib. Prepare your ad libs in advance and use them accordingly. But also be prepared to play off other speakers or the audience or some incident or feature of the room. Be alert to your surroundings. Fourth, whenever you give a speech, you'll find that you actually give three speeches: the one you prepare, the one you actually deliver, and the one you wish you had made. A lot of times after a speech, I think, *Let's get everybody back in their seats. I just thought of a great line I should've said.*"

★ ★ ★

George McGovern

A Good Man Speaking Well

George McGovern, the Democratic nominee for president in 1972, discovered his leadership ability through public speaking. He told me, "My high school English teacher said I had a talent, both in literary expression and in speaking. She introduced me to the high school debate coach, who transformed me from a somewhat shy and reticent student into a more confident and persuasive public speaker."

McGovern drew inspiration from the classics. He told me, "The Roman orator Marcus Fabius Quintilian once defined an orator as 'a good man speaking well.' You must first become a good man or a good woman before you are worth listening to as a speaker. It's the same way with other activities. A good teacher is a good person teaching well. A good coach is a good person coaching well. A good parent is a good person parenting well. I encourage people, especially young people, to become good people first, then become good speakers. The life well lived is its own reward."

In college, young George McGovern was elected class president and won a statewide speaking competition with a talk called "My Brother's Keeper." He concluded, "It was only when I saw myself as a speaker that I realized I was a leader."

★ ★ ★

Alvin Dark

"I'd Delegate"

Alvin Dark is a former shortstop and manager who played for five National League teams from 1946 to 1960. I have often visited him and his wife at their home in Easley, South Carolina. During one visit, I sat at their breakfast table and said, "Alvin, if you had your baseball management career to do over again, what would you do differently?"

"I'd delegate," he said. "I'd make much better use of my coaches. When I was managing, I did everything myself. My coaches had titles and job descriptions, but I thought I had to be the pitching coach and the hitting coach and on and on. If I could start again, I would give my coaches a whole lot more freedom and responsibility so that they could do their jobs. I wouldn't try to do it all myself."

★ ★ ★

Joe Namath

"Coach Bryant Taught Me a Lesson"

Legendary NFL quarterback Joe Namath played for Alabama's Bear Bryant from 1962 to 1964. By his own admission, Namath was the kind of player who tried Coach Bryant's soul.

During the 1963 season, when Namath was a junior quarterback, the young athlete broke training by going into a tavern. When Coach Bryant learned of the infraction, he faced a tough decision. Namath was Alabama's star quarterback. Any action that took Namath off the field would be unpopular with the fans and the other players. But Coach Bryant wasn't in that job to win popularity contests. He was there to build character and train young leaders. He decided to suspend Namath for the last two games of the season—including the 1964 Sugar Bowl.

"When Coach suspended me," Namath told me, "it was very hard on him. We were at his home, discussing the situation, and he just fell back on the bed. I was scared, really scared. I asked if he was okay, and he said yes. He sat up and said, 'Well, Joe,

I'm going to have to go ahead and suspend you.' He told me to report to his office at one p.m.

"When I got there, Coach and all his assistants were standing in the foyer. Coach said, 'My coaches and I had a meeting. Some of them think there's another way to go about this issue, but to me, that's not the right way to go. I'll retire before that.'

"I was so embarrassed that I had caused this," Namath told me. "I pleaded, 'Coach, don't do that.' But Coach Bryant said, 'We're going to have to move you out of the dorm. If you want to leave Alabama, I'll help find another place for you to go. If you want to stay and follow the rules and do everything the way I want it done, you can come back to spring practice.'

"I did go back in the spring, and I discovered that I was listed as the fifth-string quarterback. I moved up the charts very gradually. Coach Bryant taught me a lesson that stays with me to this day: No one is indispensable; no one is above the rules. And when you break the rules, you don't just hurt yourself. You hurt your teammates, your coaches, your fans, everybody."

★ ★ ★

Phil Jackson

Motivate and Inspire

Phil Jackson is one of the greatest coaches in NBA history and a longtime friend. He now gets to try his hand as a front office executive, having just been named president of basketball operations for the New York Knicks. A number of players Jackson coached later wore Magic jerseys, so I got to hear from his former players exactly how much they appreciated his ability to motivate and inspire.

At Christmas and other times of the year, Jackson would buy books and other gifts for his players. He would never buy books by the case and pass out fifteen copies of the same book. Instead, he would carefully select fifteen individual books, each targeted to an individual player's unique personality. Each gift was selected for the inspirational impact it would have on that player.

He always asked himself, "How can I motivate and inspire each of my players to step up to the next level?" His eleven NBA championship rings prove that he knew what he was doing.

Jackson once told me how one of his coaches motivated him to take responsibility as a leader on the team. "When I was a senior at the University of North Dakota," he said, "my coach was Bill Fitch. I was captain of the team. But at one point, Bill had to take the job away from me. We were playing a game in Chicago, and I went out with some friends to Rush Street. I got back to the hotel after curfew, so Bill took away my captaincy. He said, 'You won't be captain again until you prove to me you deserve it.' Bill made me prove to him that I had the self-discipline to be captain. In time, I earned my job back, and we went on to a successful season. Bill Fitch gave me a lesson in discipline that has helped me throughout my life."

★ ★ ★

Jack Ramsay

"The Authority to Make Mistakes"

I owe my long career in the NBA to Jack Ramsay.

John "Jack" Ramsay is best known for coaching the Portland Trail Blazers to the 1977 NBA title and for his broadcasting work, largely for ESPN. He was inducted into the Basketball Hall of Fame in 1992.

My first contact with Ramsay came in 1968, when he was the general manager of the Philadelphia 76ers and I was in my fourth season as the general manager of the Spartanburg Phillies.

I walked into my office and saw a phone message slip on my desk. It said I had received a call from Jack Ramsay, and I was to call him back at a number in Inglewood, California. The only Jack Ramsay I had ever heard of was in Philadelphia, but this number was in California. I was sure it couldn't be *that* Jack Ramsay. But when I called the number, I found out it *was* that Jack Ramsay. To this day, I don't know how he heard of me or who gave him my phone number.

"I'm in LA," he said, "to work out the details of our trade with the Lakers. We'll be getting Darrall Imhoff, Archie Clark, and Jerry Chambers in exchange for Wilt Chamberlain. The trade will be announced later today. I'm going to coach the 76ers this season, in addition to my general manager duties. We need a business manager, and from what I hear, you're the guy we need. Would you like the job?"

"I sure would!"

"Good. Come to Philadelphia in a few days. We'll work out the details."

For most of my life, I'd had my heart set on a career in baseball, and suddenly I had a chance at a career in professional basketball. I went to Philadelphia, and Ramsay interviewed me and gave me the job. Because of that phone call in 1968, I've spent the past five decades in the NBA.

Though Ramsay was my boss at the 76ers, he gave me a lot of leeway and decision-making authority. Years later, he explained to me his views on developing young leaders. "When you are training young leaders," he said, "you need to give them the authority to make decisions—and even make mistakes. No second-guessing. If a young leader feels his boss might swoop down and undo his decisions at any moment, he won't feel he's really leading. This undercuts his motivation to lead. Young leaders need to have a sense of genuine authority—within reasonable limits, of course. We need to stand back, let them make their decisions, and let them deal with the consequences of those decisions. Demonstrate approval when they do well, hold them accountable when they fail, and express confidence in them, win, lose, or draw."

★ ★ ★

Colin Powell

"Take Care of Your Troops"

In June 2005, I attended the twenty-fifth anniversary celebration of the Washington Speakers Bureau. Near the end of the evening, I took a trip to the dessert table and found myself within arm's reach of retired general and former secretary of state Colin Powell. In fact, we were both reaching for the same éclair.

"General Powell," I said, "I'm Pat Williams of the Orlando Magic. My son Bobby has just become a minor league manager in the Washington Nationals farm system. He just called me and told me he's eager to do everything he can to succeed. What leadership advice would you have for my son?"

The general said, "Tell your son, 'Take care of your troops.' And tell him, 'Keep your mouth shut and do your job.'" He turned to leave, then he added over his shoulder, "And tell him, 'Stay focused on this job. Don't worry about your next job.'"

And with that, he was out the door.

With Powell's words still echoing in my mind, I took a napkin from the dessert table, pulled out my pen, and wrote down his insights—a twenty-second leadership course from one of the great military leaders of our time. The next morning, I photocopied that napkin and mailed it to Bobby.

★ ★ ★

Doug Collins

A Lesson I Learned

Doug Collins was drafted by the 76ers in 1973. I arrived there a year later as the general manager, so Collins and I were together in Philadelphia for a number of years. Collins had an ongoing battle with foot and ankle problems, including stress fractures in the bones of his feet. He wanted to play, and these physical issues were very hard for him.

On one occasion, I was talking to a sportswriter about the latest foot injury Collins had suffered. I said to the writer, "Doug obviously has a low pain threshold." The reporter quoted that line in his story. I didn't think much of it until the next day when Collins showed up at my desk very upset.

"What right do you have to talk to the media about my pain threshold?" he said. "I'm the only one who knows about my ability to take pain."

I instantly realized I had misspoken. I had said "pain threshold" (which literally means one's ability to withstand pain) when what I had in mind was Collins's susceptibility to fractures. A person can be prone to physical injuries, such as fractures, and still have a very high tolerance for pain. The fact that Collins had spent a lot of time playing with his feet and ankles taped up when he probably should have been off his feet testifies to a very *high* pain threshold.

I had blown it—big-time. I apologized to Collins and told him I had learned an important lesson and it would never happen again. And it hasn't.

As a result of that incident, I learned that a leader should never comment in a way that seems to criticize or diminish a player's endurance, perseverance, or mental toughness. Saying an athlete can't tolerate pain well is an insult to his character and even his manhood. It was a careless, insensitive thing to say.

That was a teachable moment for me. I learned an important lesson about taking care of my troops.

Sparky Anderson

"Be Nice to People"

In 1965, when I was the twenty-four-year-old general manager of the Spartanburg Phillies, a new manager joined the Cardinals farm club in Rock Hill, South Carolina. His name was George "Sparky" Anderson.

Anderson had played in the big leagues one year as an infielder. Recently retired from playing, he had just started his managing career. Since we were both in the Western Carolinas League, we saw each other frequently and became acquainted. I had no way of knowing at that time that he would go on to become the third winningest manager in Major League Baseball history behind Connie Mack and John McGraw.

During those early years, Anderson and I competed ferociously, yet we were always good friends. He went on from Rock Hill to Cincinnati, then to Detroit. He had a legendary career, a Hall of Fame career. Our paths crossed many times over the next four decades, and Anderson could not have been more gracious. He'd always point me out to friends and say, "There's Pat Williams! He and I battled each other in the minor leagues in South Carolina!"

Anderson once told me that he learned his positive, joyful approach to life from his father. "My dad was a man of character who taught me how to act," he said. "He didn't tell me. He showed me. He was kind and decent to everyone. When I was eleven years old, he said, 'George, there's one thing that will make a big difference in your life, and it will never cost you a dime, and that is to be nice to people.'"

I always felt uplifted when I saw Anderson in spring training or on the road somewhere, and I was deeply saddened when he passed away in late 2010. He spread joy wherever he went, and that left a deep imprint on me.

★ ★ ★

Rich DeVos

Leadership Is Love

In August 1997, I attended an RDV Sports meeting in Grand Rapids, Michigan. RDV Sports owner Rich DeVos was still recovering from a complicated heart transplant in London, so he joined us by teleconferencing. Though he was present only via a big-screen television, his personal warmth dominated the meeting.

The item on our agenda was the downsizing of our team store, the Magic Fan Attic. It meant that sixteen jobs would be eliminated. We debated the issue for twenty minutes, and DeVos finally put the matter in focus. "This funeral has gone on long enough," he said. "It's time for the burial. So tell me what happens to those sixteen employees. Remember, I want each one of them taken care of. You can relocate them in the organization, give them good severance checks, or help them find jobs, but I want them taken care of. Understood?"

We understood.

DeVos didn't personally know any of those sixteen people,

but he loved them. He had compassion for each one because love is a leadership skill. Love is not a feeling—it's a decision. You don't have to have a warm, fuzzy emotion in order to love someone. All you have to do is seek what's best for them, just as DeVos sought what was best for the sixteen employees of the Magic Fan Attic.

Love is a learnable skill, and every leader can learn it. If you lead 'em, you've got to love 'em.

★ ★ ★

Hal Urban

"Do Everything in Love"

I once had Hal Urban on my Orlando radio show to talk about his book *The 10 Commandments of Common Sense*. He said, "When I was in college, I played basketball for two coaches. The first one was supportive and encouraging and never missed a chance to give positive feedback. The second one was always angry, had a foul mouth, and frequently humiliated his players. He never gave us any positive feedback. Obviously, I played much better for the first coach.

"As leaders, we need to catch people doing things right, then build on that. Too many young people hear more about what they do wrong than what they do right. No matter how old we are, we thrive on positive feedback.

"I recently came across a verse of Scripture that I had read many times before—1 Corinthians 16:14. This time, it spoke to me in a new way. It says, 'Do everything in love.' I thought, 'Everything? What would my life look like if I did everything in love?' So as I set off on my book tour, I made up my mind that in all my interactions with airline attendants, hotel clerks, waitresses, everybody, I would do everything in love. I tried it, and when I returned home, I told my wife, 'That was the best week I've ever had!'"

Urban's experiences inspired me. I had a three-day trip coming up, so I tried the same experiment. With every person I met along the way, I tried to serve that person in love. I talked to people and found out about their families, their interests, their plans, their dreams. When people assisted me in my travels or hotel stays, I tried to repay their kindness. When I returned home, I told my wife, Ruth, "That was the best three-day trip I've ever had!"

★ ★ ★

Tommy Lasorda

Canned, Evaporated Wisdom

Tommy Lasorda spent more than sixty years in various roles with the Brooklyn and Los Angeles Dodgers. He was inducted into the Baseball Hall of Fame in 1997 and managed the gold-medal-winning USA team at the 2000 Sydney Summer Olympics.

He once told me a story about baseball players—and cows. "One day when I was fifteen years old," he said, "my mom brought home a bag of groceries and set it on the kitchen counter. I pawed through that bag to see if she'd bought any foods I liked, and I noticed a can of Carnation evaporated milk. I read the slogan printed on the can: 'Contented cows give better milk.'

"I've remembered that slogan throughout my career. I adopted that approach as a manager. Every time I managed a team—whether it was the Ogden, Utah, Dodgers in 1965 or the Los Angeles Dodgers in 1995—I believed that contented ballplayers give better performances. That slogan guided all my management decisions."

★ ★ ★

Truett Cathy

"Honest and Successful at the Same Time"

I once shared a platform in Atlanta with Truett Cathy, founder of the Chick-fil-A restaurant chain. We were speaking to an audience of high school kids. Truett spoke first, and I sat in rapt fascination, taking notes, as he spoke in that deep, rolling Georgia accent.

One of Truett's memorable lines was "You can be honest and successful at the same time." It occurred to me that young people don't hear that message often enough. Instead, they hear that you need to do whatever it takes to win. Truett not only says that honesty and success go hand in hand but also lives it and proves it every day by the way he conducts his business.

★ ★ ★

Vince Lombardi

"I Love the Man"

Willie Davis was a dominant defensive end for the Green Bay Packers during the Vince Lombardi era. I once asked Davis to tell me about his last conversation with Coach Lombardi in 1970, after Davis had retired from football. Here's what he told me.

He was at San Diego Stadium for an exhibition game, the New York Giants versus the Chargers. During the game, Giants owner Duke Mara told him that Coach Lombardi was in a DC hospital dying of cancer.

Davis rushed out of the stadium, drove straight to LAX, and took a night flight to Washington. He grabbed a cab to Georgetown University Hospital and was met there by Mrs. Lombardi. She led him into Coach Lombardi's hospital room.

"That was the only time I ever saw Coach Lombardi not in control," Davis said. "You should have seen him smile. He didn't have much voice, but he whispered, 'Willie, you were a great player. That was the best deal I ever made.' He started to cry, and I did too. I was in the room for only about two minutes. Then

Mrs. Lombardi led me out and said, 'He gets very emotional when the old Packers come to visit.'"

Davis flew cross-country for just two minutes with his old coach. He felt it was time and money well spent. As he was getting into a cab to return home, reporters asked him, "Why did you fly across the country to see Coach Lombardi?"

"Because," Davis said, "he made me feel important. I love the man."

Part 3

★ ★ ★

Family and Friends

★ ★ ★

Michael Jordan

"A Product of My Mom and Dad"

In 2001, I was in Boston at the same time Michael Jordan and the Washington Wizards were playing the Boston Celtics. Before the game, I went down to the locker room to visit with Jordan.

"Hey, Williams," he said, "I saw you on television this morning talking about the book. You know, you're telling all my stories!"

I grinned and said, "You know, Mike, your stories are getting raves from readers all over the country. People say, 'When you see Mike, thank him for being a role model.'"

He grinned and said, "I'm just a product of my mom and dad. Everything I am today is a result of the way James and Deloris Jordan raised me and all the things they taught me."

★ ★ ★

Oprah Winfrey

A Comforter in a Crisis

On Memorial Day weekend 2000, a terrible tragedy invaded Julius Erving's family. The family was having a cookout, and Erving's youngest son, Cory, went out to the store to buy bread—and never returned.

It was every parent's worst nightmare. Cory had simply disappeared without a trace. Was he the victim of a crime or an accident? Had he run away without leaving word?

Erving went before the news cameras and pleaded for his son to come home and for anyone with information to bring it forward. He also asked me to be the family spokesperson in dealing with the media, which I readily agreed to do.

On July 6, more than a month after Cory was last seen alive, his body was found in a car submerged in a pond less than a mile from the Erving home. He had taken a shortcut along a dirt road—a route he had taken many times before—and had lost control of the car. He was either killed outright in the crash or was unable to escape.

Cory's funeral drew hundreds of friends of the Erving family, including Oprah Winfrey. As part of the Erving family contingent, I was with Julius, his wife Turquoise, their children, and Oprah. The woman known as "the queen of all media" was not there in a public capacity but in an intensely intimate capacity. She was there as a comforter.

I was very impressed and deeply moved to see Oprah in that setting, helping Julius and his family process their raw emotions. She spoke to them, embraced them, and wept softly with them. She set an example of how to handle oneself in a crisis with hurting people.

I talked to her briefly, but she devoted herself to reaching out to the Erving family. I came away from that experience with a new respect for the depths of Oprah's empathy and compassion for others.

★ ★ ★

Bill Bright

"Don't Forget the Love"

When our children were of school age, I had dinner with Campus Crusade for Christ founder Bill Bright and his wife, Vonette, after they had moved their headquarters to Orlando. Bill was fascinated by our large brood—at that time, four birth children and fourteen children by international adoption. He wanted to know how we managed our big household.

I told Bill about some of the rules and discipline we instilled in order to keep our big family functioning smoothly. Bill listened patiently.

Then, very gently, he said, "That's all very good, Pat, but don't forget the love."

I always remembered that wise advice. Yes, a household needs order, but kids need love. While setting up your rules and discipline, don't forget the love.

Allan Houston

The Fundamentals of Life

I once had former Knicks and Pistons shooting guard Allan Houston as a guest on my Orlando radio show. He told me he learned the meaning of fatherhood and manhood from his own father—and from his son.

"Every son wants to be like his dad," Houston told me. "My seven-year-old son has a toy shaving kit he brings into the bathroom when I'm shaving. He takes off his shirt and stands in front of the sink next to me and pretends to shave. That's a reminder that he's watching me and learning what it means to be a man. And it reminds me that I learned all about being a man from my own father.

"My dad was a basketball coach, and he's not shy about telling people where I got my jump shot! He taught me the fundamentals of the game. He knew I'd have an advantage against my opponents if I was prepared and knew what to expect on the court. And he taught me the fundamentals of life so I'd be equipped to deal with every situation life might throw at me.

"My father taught me that making money is not as important as how you treat people while you're making it. He taught me the fundamentals of life, and now I'm teaching them to my son."

Jameer Nelson

A Father's Legacy

Jameer Nelson is the starting point guard for the Orlando
Magic. He grew up in Chester, Pennsylvania. His father, Floyd
"Pete" Nelson, was a welder who maintained tugboats at a
shop on the Delaware River. In 2007, Pete Nelson was reported
missing. Jameer went home to take part in the search for his
fifty-seven-year-old father.

Had his dad been kidnapped? Would there be a ransom de-
mand? Had his dad suffered heatstroke or a heart attack? Had
he fallen into the water? The hardest part was not knowing.

Two days after Pete's disappearance, fishermen found his
body in the river. The cause of death was never determined.
Pete was a retired Marine, a Vietnam combat veteran. Jameer
and his brothers called him "Pops." They were going to miss
their dad's incredible barbecue, his wild tall tales, his laughter,
and his wisdom.

One of the most important lessons Jameer learned from his
dad was a strong work ethic. After Jameer achieved stardom in
the NBA, he tried to talk his dad into retiring. "Why keep working so hard, Pops?" he said. "Why not let me make things easier
for you?" But Pete liked working with his hands. He wasn't ready
to retire. That relentless work ethic spoke volumes to Jameer.

Pete's funeral was held at St. Luke's Community Christian
Church in Chester. Jameer's teammates and the Magic staff
went to Chester for the funeral. One of Jameer's Magic teammates, Dwight Howard, told the congregation, "We've come to

show that we're a team, we're a family. Jameer may have lost his earthly father, but nothing can take away his heavenly Father."

The officiating minister, Bishop Anthony Hanna Sr., was Pete's son-in-law. He said, "We're all asking, 'Why did Pete Nelson have to die?' I'll tell you why. If he hadn't died, you wouldn't be in church today, would you? He died to make you better, to make you stronger, to make you wiser. And the only way for you to be better, stronger, and wiser is through Jesus Christ."

After the funeral, Jameer told reporters, "My dad is still with me. He'll always be with me." When Jameer's father died, he left behind a life-changing legacy that lives on.

★ ★ ★

Doc Rivers

An "Unrealistic" Goal

Before Glenn "Doc" Rivers became an NBA coach, he enjoyed a thirteen-year career as a point guard in the NBA. His parents, Chicago policeman Grady Rivers and his wife, Bettye, taught him to believe in himself and his dreams. When Glenn was in the third grade, his teacher tried to shrink his dreams down to size. The teacher had the students come up to the chalkboard and write what they planned to be when they grew up. Young Glenn took the chalk and wrote "professional basketball player."

The teacher told him that was an unrealistic goal. She erased the words Glenn had written on the board and said, "Think of something else you'd like to do and write that on the board—lawyer, doctor, shoe clerk, anything."

Glenn took the chalk and again wrote "professional basketball player."

The teacher erased his words again and gave him one last chance.

Glenn wrote—well, you know what he wrote. So the teacher sent him to the principal's office. After hearing the boy's side of the story, the principal sided with Glenn. So did his parents.

And maybe that's why Doc Rivers has had such a long NBA career.

* ★ *

Laura Bush

A Dad-Shaped Hole in the Soul

In April 2005, the National Fatherhood Initiative (NFI) honored country music star Buddy Jewell, Fox News analyst Fred Barnes, Atlanta Falcons defensive back Allen Rossum, and me at its annual Fatherhood Awards Gala. It was an award for dads who exemplify committed fatherhood.

I figured someone at NFI had heard about my nineteen kids (four birth kids, fourteen adopted, one by remarriage) and said, "Well, Pat Williams at least deserves an award for quantity, if not quality." As I contemplated the award I was about to receive, I was keenly aware of the times I had failed as a father, times I should have been more strict (or less), times I should have listened more, and times I should have given better advice.

The event was held in the grand ballroom of the Willard InterContinental Hotel in DC, just two blocks from the White House, and our speaker for the evening was First Lady Laura Bush. I looked around the ballroom and thought, *What am I doing here? I'm a pair of old sneakers in a roomful of tuxedoes!*

It was quite an emotional evening. R&B star Cincere performed a song called "Daddy" with a kids' chorus that sang, "Daddy, Daddy, Daddy, come home!" I had to dab at my eyes during that one!

Then Laura Bush spoke. "Across America," she said, "twenty-four million children live apart from their father. Forty percent of these children haven't seen their father in the last year. As Roland Warren has said, 'Kids have a hole in their soul the shape of their dad.' Statistics show that when children grow up without a mom and dad at home, they're more likely to fall behind in school, more likely to experiment with drugs and alcohol, and more likely to be in trouble with the law. . . . The evidence is clear: Children need fathers in their lives."

She also talked about a Milwaukee program called Today's Dads that mentors teen fathers to become good fathers, and she talked about a young man she had met named Ken. He had grown up with drug-addicted parents and surrounded by crime. When his girlfriend became pregnant, Ken decided to give his little boy a better life than he'd had. With the help of the Today's Dads program, Ken walked away from the drug trade and took a job delivering pizzas. By working nights, he was able to stay home with the baby during the day. Selling drugs was easy money; delivering pizzas is hard work, but, said Laura Bush, "Ken wants to be a man and a father."

Kids deserve hands-on, committed fathers. No matter what a man does for a living, if he has children, fatherhood is his number one job.

★ ★ ★

Paul Simon

The Poet and His Son

In January 2014, I was at the arena for a home game when word spread that musician Paul Simon was in the building. In my younger days, Simon and Garfunkel were my musical heroes. Songs like "The Sound of Silence," "Mrs. Robinson," "Bridge over Troubled Water," and "The Boxer" formed the soundtrack of my early adult years. There has never been a musical duo like Simon and Garfunkel, and their songs, with their beautiful harmonies and powerful messages, never age.

Somebody pointed Paul Simon out to me and said, "There he is in the front row—the guy in the blue ball cap."

During a time-out, I slipped over to where he was seated and introduced myself. He greeted me warmly and introduced his teenage son seated next to him. He explained that he and his son were huge NBA fans and were visiting NBA arenas across the country.

"I grew up with your music," I said, "and it's a real treat to have you in our arena."

"Thank you, Pat," he said. "I'll be back in March. I'm doing a concert in this very building."

Our chat was brief, and the most important part was not what Paul Simon said to me but what I saw with my own eyes: an involved, committed father, investing time in his relationship with his son. I never get tired of seeing a dad doing what he was put on earth to do, being a guide, friend, and hero to his son.

★ ★ ★

John Maxwell

Learning Leadership in the Home

John Maxwell's name is synonymous with leadership. The author of more than sixty books, including *The 21 Irrefutable Laws of Leadership*, Maxwell has devoted most of his career to teaching the principles of leadership through his speaking and writing. In 1985, he founded the INJOY Group, which produces leadership seminars and conferences. I once asked him how he came to be fascinated with leadership.

"I learned about leadership in the home," he told me. "My father believed in personal growth and leadership. When we were little, Mom and Dad read to us constantly. At each stage of development, my parents introduced us to new books. By the time I was in the third grade, I was required to read for thirty minutes every day. At first, I read stories from the Bible. As I grew, my parents gave me other books to read, such as *The Power of Positive Thinking* by Norman Vincent Peale and *How to Win Friends and Influence People* by Dale Carnegie.

"My parents picked the books, and they paid me part of my allowance to read them. Each night at dinner, we discussed our reading. We were encouraged to share not only the facts we had learned but also our opinion. I read every weekday until I graduated from high school."

★ ★ ★

Mike Shula

Age Isn't Important

I first met NFL coach Don Shula in 1958, when I was a high school football player and Shula was an assistant coach at the University of Virginia. Today, Don's son, Mike Shula, is the offensive coordinator for the Carolina Panthers. During an interview with Mike, he told me how he learned the fundamentals of leadership.

"In grade school, we would choose sides for pickup games," he said. "I always did the choosing. The desire to be a leader came early in life, and my father and brother taught me how to be a leader in football and in life. Most importantly, they taught me how a leader should treat people.

"I started coaching at age twenty-two, and the guys I coached were as old as thirty-three. It took me ten years to reach an age where the people I coached were younger than me. I quickly realized that your age isn't nearly as important as the type of person you are. If you have wisdom, confidence, and experience, people will place their trust in you and follow you anywhere."

★ ★ ★

Harry, Skip, and Chip Caray

A Family Legacy

I feel like I've known the Carays all my life.

I grew up as a baseball fan listening to the great Harry Caray, the voice of the St. Louis Cardinals on Radio KMOX, a station that boomed out all over the country. When I was with the Bulls in the early 1970s, Harry was the voice of the White Sox. I got to know him and always enjoyed the times I spent with him.

I left the Bulls in 1973 to serve as the general manager of the Atlanta Hawks. And who was the radio voice of the Atlanta Hawks? None other than Skip Caray, Harry's son. I was in Atlanta for only a year, but I enjoyed getting to know Skip and hearing him do the play-by-play for the Hawks.

After a twelve-year run with the Philadelphia 76ers, I moved to Orlando in 1986 to build the Magic from scratch. We started acquiring players, designing uniforms, and auditioning broadcast announcers. One of the announcers who applied was twenty-four-year-old Chip Caray—Skip's son, Harry's grandson—and we hired him.

Chip had a deep love for his legendary grandfather. "I didn't get to be with my grandfather as much as I would have liked," Chip once told me. "He was in Chicago, and I grew up in St. Louis, but when I'd see him on television, I felt like it was personal, like I was getting a grandfatherly hug from him. He was the ultimate fan, shouting 'Holy cow!' at every homer, singing 'Take Me Out to the Ballgame,' and signing autographs. I learned the love of the game from Granddad."

One time, all three generations of Carays—Harry, Skip, and Chip—were in the broadcast booth at Wrigley Field in Chicago announcing a Cubs game. Having a father, son, and grandson all announcing the same game had to be a first and only in the annals of baseball.

One night in February 1998, Chip was on the far side of the arena, getting ready for a Magic broadcast. He saw me and sent an intern over to me with a handwritten note. I took the note from the intern, unfolded it, and read, "Granddad passed away today." That's how I learned that Harry had left us. Living in retirement in Palm Springs, he'd taken a bad fall in a restaurant, striking his head. He died just a few days short of his eighty-fourth birthday. He is missed, but he has left us a legacy through his son and grandson.

★ ★ ★

Robin Roberts

"Isn't Sports Great?"

I have two friends named Robin Roberts. One is the cohost of *Good Morning America* on ABC. The *other* Robin Roberts was a boyhood idol of mine—a pitcher who played most of his career with the Philadelphia Phillies. He and I became good friends after he retired to Tampa. He passed away in 2010.

Roberts had a great enthusiasm for sports and for life. One Monday morning, he called me up. It had been an incredibly rich weekend for sports fans. Northwestern had upset Notre Dame in football. There had been a number of great NFL matchups. The baseball pennant races were raging. So Roberts said to me, "Patty, isn't sports great?!"

And I thought, *He's right. Sports are great!*

Sports keep the temperature of America up high. Sports fill us with enthusiasm for our teams. We root for our hometowns, our schools, our teams, our heroes. We rejoice when our teams win. We get mad when they lose. Our passion for competition helps make us who we are as a uniquely American people. Before every game, we sing the National Anthem and cheer for our American ideals. Sports bind us together in our love for the game, whether the game is baseball, basketball, football, hockey, soccer, tennis, or golf.

The late Nelson Mandela put it beautifully: "Sport has the power to change the world. It has the power to inspire. It has the power to unite people in a way that little else does. It speaks to youth in a language they understand. Sport can create hope where there was once only despair."[3]

Roberts loved not only sports but also his wife, Mary, and their four sons. One day, Roberts chatted with his friend Pat Peppler, who had a long coaching career in the NFL. They talked about the life of a professional athlete, with all the temptations of playing on the road. They recalled some of the players they had known who had destroyed their marriages by yielding to those temptations.

"Those vices are all around you when you're on the road," Roberts said. "It's all within easy reach. But that's not for me. I couldn't do that to Mary."

Roberts was as devoted to his family as he was to baseball. When he died at age eighty-three, he left a legacy of faithfulness and honor to his sons—and to us all.

* ★ *

Brian Shaw

An Inner Strength

Brian Shaw is the head coach of the Denver Nuggets. He spent four years of an exciting fifteen-year playing career as a guard for the Orlando Magic. His alley-oop passes to Shaq were sheer poetry.

Early one Saturday morning in June 1993, Shaw's father, Charles, was driving the family's Jeep Cherokee along Interstate 15 south of Las Vegas. Also in the car were Brian's mother, Barbara; his twenty-four-year-old sister, Monica; and Monica's one-year-old daughter, Brianna. Either Charles fell asleep or the Cherokee was run off the road by an unknown driver—no one knows for sure. The car flipped off the road and landed upside down. Shaw's dad, mom, and sister were killed; only his little niece Brianna survived. In that instant, Shaw lost nearly all of his family.

Almost two thousand people packed the six-hundred-seat Taylor Memorial United Methodist Church in Oakland for the memorial service. Shaw stood before the packed sanctuary, and in a voice that was firm but emotional, he delivered a moving tribute to his parents and his sister. The other mourners both laughed and cried along with this courageous young man.

"My family gave me an inner strength to deal with this," he later said. "I try to be positive about the memories, the many good times. Those thoughts are uplifting, even with the physical separation. I feel like my family is still present with me, watching over me. And I really want to make them proud."

Brian Shaw is a warm, gentle, humble human being in a business in which overstuffed egos are the norm. It's a privilege to know him and to watch him coach and live this life. He is a living legacy and a tribute to his family.

★ ★ ★

Bobby Richardson

A Friend I Can Trust

When my first marriage was crumbling in 1994, I was utterly devastated. I felt an overwhelming sense of shame and humiliation, and I kept our separation a secret even from my closest friends.

In July 1995, I was in South Carolina for a speaking engagement. I stopped in Sumter to have dinner with Bobby Richardson, Yankees star second baseman from 1955 to 1966, and his wife, Betsy. I first met Bobby when I was a young Minor League Baseball executive in Spartanburg, South Carolina, and he had always been a friend and encourager.

After dinner, we were talking, and I felt God urging me to open up and tell my friends about my collapsing marriage. As soon as the thought occurred to me, I began arguing with myself: *No! Don't say anything! It's too embarrassing! What would Bobby and Betsy think of me if they knew I was heading for divorce?*

But then I felt God's Spirit saying to me, "It's okay. Trust them. Trust me. Tell them."

So I took a deep breath and told them that my wife had left me and that I felt completely shattered. I was amazed at their response. Instead of the rejection or disappointment I feared, they surrounded me with acceptance and encouragement. They prayed with me, and I left their home feeling completely uplifted by them—and by God.

I had a similar experience in 2011, after I was diagnosed with multiple myeloma. I hadn't announced the diagnosis publicly yet. Bobby came to town on business, and some mutual friends invited Bobby and me to dinner. Boy, did I need that!

I told Bobby about my diagnosis, and once again I felt surrounded by Christian love and prayer. It meant so much coming from Bobby Richardson, who was not only a great baseball player I admired but also a great friend I could always trust.

★ ★ ★

Linda Evans

If You Don't Have Peace Within . . .

A few years ago, I was in Birmingham, Alabama, in a building complex with half a dozen radio stations lining the hall. I finished my interview at one station and was heading toward the elevator when a door opened and who should be standing in front of me but the lovely Linda Evans, star of television's *Big Valley* and *Dynasty*. I fumbled and stammered and introduced myself, and she could not have been sweeter.

Sometime later, Linda wrote her memoirs in an ingenious way, merging her life story with a cookbook—all her favorite recipes. I invited her to be a guest on my radio show, and we had a fascinating conversation about her show business career and cooking.

During our chat, she shared a powerful insight, saying, "I've seen so many people chasing happiness through success in show business. But if you don't have a peace and satisfaction within, all the money, fame, and success won't give it to you. There are a lot of people in Hollywood who seem to have it made, but being successful doesn't mean you have it made. Happiness comes from within."

She put me so completely at ease that I surprised myself by boldly inviting myself to her home! "Linda," I said, "if I'm ever out your way, I'd like to come over for dinner."

"Well, you just do that!" she said. "I'll cook you up a real nice meal."

I haven't taken her up on it yet, but one of these days I will!

Part 4

★ ★ ★

Impact
and Influence

Keith Tower and Rich DeVos

The Gift

Six eleven forward and center Keith Tower joined the Magic roster in 1993, at the inception of the Shaq era. He played a limited but important backup role with the team. Rich DeVos and the DeVos family had purchased the Magic in late 1991, and Rich delighted in giving players a special gift at Christmastime. For Christmas 1993, he gave each player a beautiful Bible with the player's name embossed on the cover.

When Tower opened his gift, his first thought (as he later told me) was, *Man, what a lame gift!* Tower would have been happier with some sort of electronic device. He took the Bible home, set it on a shelf, and ignored it for the next few years.

In 1996, Tower joined the Milwaukee Bucks. Before training camp, he wanted to take something with him to occupy his downtime. He had plenty of electronic gadgets, but he was bored with them. He took down the Bible, blew off the dust, and tossed it in his suitcase. Then he took off for Milwaukee.

One night in his hotel room, Tower took out his Bible, began reading, and became convicted of his need to follow God. He prayed and invited Jesus Christ to take control of his life.

After retiring from the game, Tower and former Magic

teammate Andrew DeClercq cofounded HighPoint Church in Orlando. The church began with four people meeting for a Bible study in DeClercq's home and grew into a dynamic congregation with hundreds of members. And it all began with Rich DeVos's "lame gift" of a Bible at Christmastime.

★ ★ ★

Pete Maravich

"If You Don't Save Me, Nothing Will"

I arrived in 1973 as the general manager of the Atlanta Hawks, and my assignment was to resuscitate a dying team. The talent-laden Hawks had been play-off contenders for more than a decade but had never reached the top. As I assumed my duties, the team was poised for a promising season. But the team quickly unraveled, losing sixteen of the first seventeen road games after New Year's Day. We had great players, a great coach, yet the team couldn't get in sync.

Coach Cotton Fitzsimmons tried every trick in the book to motivate his players, but nothing worked. His biggest challenge was our superstar guard, "Pistol" Pete Maravich. Brash and confident, Maravich dazzled crowds with his behind-the-back dribble and pinpoint shooting. But Fitzsimmons couldn't get Maravich to play within the team's system. Maravich was a thrill a minute to watch, but he refused to fly in formation. We didn't have a real team—we had one run-and-gun performer and four other guys who ran up and down the court watching Maravich shoot.

Near the end of our frustrating 1973–74 season, I talked to attorney Fred Rosenfeld, one of the owners of the New Orleans Jazz. An expansion franchise, the Jazz was hungry for top-drawer talent. "We're interested in Maravich," he said. "Pete went to Louisiana State, and our fans love him."

"You're dreaming," I said. "You can't afford Pete Maravich."

The fact is we wanted to trade Maravich, but to the Jazz? What could an expansion team offer in trade?

Rosenfeld kept calling, and each time he called, his offer was more creative. Finally, he called with a suggestion that was the perfect yes-yes. I had Fitzsimmons sit in as I dickered with Rosenfeld. I wanted our head coach to have the final say on any talent we acquired or lost. In the end, we got a sweet deal. New Orleans landed Maravich, and we ended up with a wealth of draft picks, all destined to be good ones.

I drove over to Maravich's condo to give him the news. A clause in his contract gave him approval over any trade. I laid out the deal we had made for him, and he was shocked. "That's it?" he said. "That's all you got for me?" But in the end, Maravich's new contract in New Orleans was very lucrative for him.

Maravich retired from the NBA in 1980, having never won a championship. He became so bitter over the emptiness of his life that he destroyed all his career memorabilia. His personal life went to pieces. He turned to alcohol and drove his sports car down country roads at 140 miles an hour hoping to kill himself.

One sleepless night in 1982, Maravich called out to God and said, "If you don't save me, nothing will. Take over my life." After he prayed that prayer, his life changed. Everyone who knew him was amazed at the transformation in his life. The old egotism and abrasiveness were replaced by a quiet humility.

After Maravich's conversion, he and I became reacquainted. He told me he attributed his lack of a championship ring to immaturity, a lack of discipline, and an unwillingness to sacrifice personal glory for the good of the team.

In 1987, Maravich was inducted into the Hall of Fame. Around that time, his father, basketball coach Press Maravich, was diagnosed with terminal cancer. Pete was with his dad during his final hours and later said that he whispered in his father's ear, "Dad, I'll be with you soon." He evidently had a premonition that his time was short.

Weeks later, Maravich was in Southern California for a radio interview with James Dobson. A longtime NBA fan, Dobson asked the former NBA star to play a pickup game with him at a church gym near the studio. Dobson was dazzled by Maravich's skills.

"You should come out of retirement," Dobson said.

"Actually," Maravich said, "this is the first time I've played in a while. I've been having chest pains for a year or so."

"How do you feel today?"

"I feel great!"

Those were Maravich's last words. Moments later, he collapsed to the floor. Dobson applied CPR while someone else called 911, but Maravich was already gone. An autopsy later disclosed a previously undetected heart defect. The coroner was surprised that Maravich had survived a strenuous ten-year NBA career with such a serious heart problem. Maravich died on January 5, 1988, at just forty years of age.

The old Pistol Pete was a difficult guy to know, work with, and deal with. His pursuit of basketball glory had left him empty and bitter, but God reached into his life and made a new man of him. I'm glad I got to know him—both the old Pistol Pete and the new man.

★ ★ ★

Wendell Kempton

Four Absolutes

When Joe Gibbs was coaching the Redskins in the 1980s, he called and asked if I could speak at a team chapel service. I had a conflict that Sunday, so I called a missionary executive I knew, Wendell Kempton, and he did the service.

Sunday night after the game, I called Kempton and asked how the service had gone. He said, "It went great, Pat. Thanks for letting me stand in for you."

"What did you speak about, Wendell?"

He told me, and what he said to the team that night has had a lifelong impact on me. He said, "I told them that there are four absolutes that you have as a Christian.

"First, you have a faith that is fixed. A biblical faith never changes. Keep your eyes on Jesus and your faith will never waver.

"Second, you have a forgiveness that is free. The Lord has forgiven all your sins. There's nothing you can do to earn forgiveness, nothing you can do to get these sins off your neck by yourself. The Lord has given you a forgiveness that cost you nothing because it cost him everything.

"Third, you've got a fellowship with the Father. You can commune with him, pray to him, listen to him, and he will speak to you in the stillness of your soul. Through prayer, you can have fellowship with the Creator of the universe.

"Fourth, you have a future that is forever. In John 5:24, we see that when the time comes, you'll be in the presence of the Lord. You'll have an eternal home with him.

"A faith that is fixed, a forgiveness that is free, a fellowship with the Father, and a future that is forever—these are the four absolutes of your faith as a Christian."

That was Kempton's message to the Redskins that day, and I told him, "Wendell, I'm going to borrow that message and use it myself."

He said, "Be my guest!"

Joe Gibbs and Wendell Kempton became close friends after that, and Kempton's talk about the four absolutes has been my go-to message ever since.

★ ★ ★

Bill Bright

Four Spiritual Laws

I committed my life to Jesus Christ in February 1968 in Spartanburg, South Carolina, largely through the influence of Campus Crusade for Christ. A young woman in a Campus Crusade singing group handed me a booklet called "The Four Spiritual Laws," and it had a big impact on my thinking. After my decision for Christ, I kept hearing the name Bill Bright, the founder of Campus Crusade for Christ.

Not long after I moved to Orlando, I heard that Campus Crusade was thinking of moving its head office from California to either Charlotte or Orlando. Bill Bright came to Orlando, and I was invited to have breakfast with him to help put Orlando's best foot forward.

I told him that his four spiritual laws had impacted my life and my faith in a big way—and I also made my pitch for Orlando. "Bill," I said, "if you want fresh-squeezed orange juice right from the tree in your backyard, you've got to move to Orlando."

Campus Crusade moved its headquarters to Orlando in 1988, and Bill became a good friend.

Bill suffered for years from pulmonary fibrosis, a chronic and progressive lung disease. Breathing became an increasingly difficult struggle for him. I once went to see him at Florida Hospital in Orlando. I found his wife, Vonette, pushing him in a wheelchair along a hospital sidewalk. I recall the date clearly— September 10, 2001, the day before the September 11 terror attacks.

I said, "Bill, how are you doing?"

Smiling behind his oxygen mask, his voice a soft whisper, he said, "Just praising the Lord." That was Bill Bright's faithful spirit in a nutshell—never complaining, always praising God.

I once visited with Vonette after Bill's death. We reminisced about Bill, and she told me of a phone call he received shortly before his death. The call was from President George W. Bush. The evangelist chatted with the leader of the free world for a few minutes, then Bill said, "Thank you for this call, Mr. President. I'm honored to receive a call from the most powerful man in the world, but soon I'm going to meet someone far greater—the King of kings and Lord of lords."

On July 19, 2003, Bill met his Lord and King.

Vonette told me about a conversation she had with her husband shortly before his death. She asked him why God allowed him to go through such suffering. Bill told her, "What I'm going through is so minor. I'm here in a bed of ease, surrounded by people who love me. Suffering is a matter of perspective. It's not pleasant, but God allows only so much—and I feel so blessed."

★ ★ ★

Roosevelt Grier

"It Doesn't Begin to Compare"

Former defensive tackle Roosevelt "Rosey" Grier of the New York Giants and Los Angeles Rams has had quite a career as a football player, actor, and speaker. He was also the man who captured and subdued the killer of Robert F. Kennedy in Los Angeles in 1968. Grier recently told me, "I look back on my life, at the things I've done and the people I've known, and as wonderful as all of that is, it doesn't begin to compare to the moment I came to know Jesus Christ as my Savior."

★ ★ ★

Tony Dungy

"Hug Them Every Chance You Get"

Tony Dungy is perhaps best known as the head coach of the Indianapolis Colts, who won Super Bowl XLI on February 4, 2007, defeating the Chicago Bears. Away from the sidelines, Dungy is committed to serving Christ and serving others. He's actively involved with Athletes in Action, Fellowship of Christian

Athletes, Big Brothers/Big Sisters, Boys and Girls Club, Prison Crusade Ministry, and many other ministries.

Dungy's faith was severely tested three days before Christmas 2005 when his eighteen-year-old son, James, was found dead in his Florida apartment. The coroner concluded that James had committed suicide. At the funeral, Dungy stood before fifteen hundred mourners and urged them never to take family for granted.

He recalled the last time he had seen his son, which was at Thanksgiving as James was leaving for the airport. "I told him, 'I'll see you later,'" he recalled. "I didn't get to hug him. I knew I'd see him again pretty soon, so it didn't really bother me very much. We talked on the phone a lot the last few days. . . . He was saying—as the guys on the team knew he would—he was saying, 'Dad, we're going to the Super Bowl, and when we do, will I be on the field?'"

At that point, he choked up, then finished his thought. "I said, 'Yeah, man. You know the hard part is getting there, but if we do, you know you're going to be on the field.' But I never got to hug him again. That's one thing I'll always think about and always remind people to do. Hug them every chance you get. Tell them you love them every chance you get because you don't know when it's going to be the last time."

After hearing Dungy's strong Christian testimony at his son's funeral, many people made a decision to follow Christ. Dungy later told a reporter, "If God had talked to me before James's death and said his death would have helped all these people, it would have saved them and healed their sins, but I would have to take your son, I would have said, 'No, I can't do that.' But God had the same choice two thousand years ago with His Son, Jesus Christ, and it paved the way for you and me to have eternal life. That's the benefit I got, that's the benefit James got, and that's the benefit you can get if you accept Jesus into your heart today as your Savior."[4]

★ ★ ★

Warren Wiersbe

The Furnace of Affliction

Warren Wiersbe became the pastor of Moody Memorial Church in Chicago while I was with the Chicago Bulls. I sat under his ministry during my final three years there, and I'm convinced there has never been a finer Bible teacher. In those days, he was just beginning to write the many important books that continue to impact the world to this day.

One time at lunch together, I told him about some frustrations in my career. I expected him to give me some answers—or at least some sympathy. Instead, he seemed positively *pleased* that I was going through adversity! "Now, Pat," he said, "don't waste your sufferings. Life is full of problems, so you might as well put them to good use."

Wiersbe left Chicago not long after that and moved to Lincoln, Nebraska, to take over the *Back to the Bible* broadcasts from founder Theodore Epp. He had a long ministry there, and he continued to live in Lincoln after his retirement from the broadcast. Every time I have a speaking engagement in Lincoln, I swing by his home for a visit and a booster shot of encouragement. I love talking to him and perusing his vast library, which occupies the entire basement level of his home.

The last time I was in Lincoln, Wiersbe and I had lunch together. He told me, "When we go to heaven, we will take with us the Bible we have in our hearts and heads. That's why it's so important to study the Bible while we are here."

I said, "What are your thoughts on heaven, Warren?"

He said, "First, I think we will teach each other and learn from each other in heaven. Second, I think there will be a point where a big screen comes down and you'll be shown a complete replaying of your life, from birth to glory. Tears will flow when you find out all that God did for you, and then an angel will come and wipe away all your tears and say, 'It's all right now. Don't worry anymore. You're home.'"

He shared one more thought with me that day. "Don't ever give up on what God can do. We are impatient, but God is so patient. He'll answer our prayers in due time if we remain patient in our requests."

I had Wiersbe on my radio show in November 2013, and he talked about the purpose of adversity in our lives. "The most important thing you have to do in life is learn to deal with difficult times," he said. "I've learned that there are four steps to dealing with adversity. First, developing the courage to face adversity. Second, developing the wisdom to understand adversity. Third, developing the strength to do what we have to do. And fourth, having the faith to wait. Nothing teaches patience like the furnace of affliction."

An hour with Warren Wiersbe is the equivalent of a semester in seminary.

Dick Bavetta

Chaos on the Court

NBA referee Dick Bavetta holds the record for most games officiated and most players ejected in a single game—ten brawling Knicks and Nuggets in an infamous game in December 2006. Bavetta once reminded me of a game he officiated in the early 1980s between the Philadelphia 76ers and the Boston Celtics in Boston. Though the game took place during my tenure, I was not in Boston Garden for that game. I'm sorry I missed it!

In those days, there were just two refs on the court, and Bavetta's partner was Jack Madden. The crowd was raucous; the rivalry was intense. Early on, Madden collided with a Celtics player, broke his leg, and was carted away, so Bavetta had to work the rest of the game by himself.

He called the two coaches together—the 76ers' Billy Cunningham and the Celtics' K. C. Jones. He said. "Let's cooperate. Okay, fellas?" The spirit of cooperation lasted about twenty seconds.

Before long, chaos reigned on the court. Bavetta had to charge Jones with a technical. Then he looked in the corner and saw Julius Erving of the 76ers and Larry Bird of the Celtics choking each other, so he ejected both. Then he charged Cunningham with a technical and tossed him out of the game. As Cunningham headed for the locker room, he was pelted and jeered by Celtics fans. Then Bavetta realized that Cunningham had received one technical, not two, so he had to go get Cunningham out of the locker room.

When the final buzzer sounded, Bavetta thought his career

was over as well as the game. He was sure there had never been a more out-of-control game in the annals of the NBA.

The next day, Cunningham was quoted in the papers praising Bavetta for having the courage to eject Erving and Bird. That commendation caused NBA officials to take notice of Bavetta. No longer was he viewed as a rookie but as a fair-minded, battle-hardened pro.

"That was the turning point of my officiating career," Bavetta told me. "I started getting choice assignments because the league started looking at me as a leader."

Bavetta's experience reminds us that we should never run from adversity, because adversity reveals what we are made of.

* ★ *

Joe Torre

"Be Vigilant!"

Longtime infielder and baseball manager Joe Torre has battled prostate cancer for years, and he knows the meaning of adversity. He became aware of my cancer battle, and when I saw him at a recent event, we chatted about cancer and encouraged each other. At the end of our conversation, we shook hands and parted. Torre took a few steps, then he turned and called back to me, "Be vigilant!"

I knew what he meant. Don't leave anything to chance with this illness. Stay on top of it. Don't let up. Fight it. Make it to all your appointments. Take your medicine on schedule. Monitor how you're feeling. Be vigilant.

I think about those words every day. That's good counsel, cancer patient or not.

★ ★ ★

Peter Gammons and Dean Smith

A Huge Day

Peter Gammons has been a prominent baseball writer for years and is now a baseball commentator on television. He went to the University of North Carolina and wrote for the student newspaper. This was during Dean Smith's tenure as the ultra-successful North Carolina basketball coach.

Gammons told me he was at his desk at the *Daily Tarheel* when the phone rang. It was Coach Smith. Recalling that phone conversation, Gammons is still amazed. "He was calling me, a student writer! Coach Smith said, 'Peter, one of the top sports-writers in the country, Frank DeFord of *Sports Illustrated*, is coming to Chapel Hill to spend the day interviewing me. I'd like you to come over and sit in on the interview, to see how he does it, so you can learn from him.'"

That was forty-some years ago, Gammons told me, and it was a huge day in his life. "Think of it," he said. "One of the greatest coaches in the history of sports thought to invite me, a student newspaper writer, to observe a great sportswriter conducting an interview. Coach Smith knew it would be helpful to me in my career. Needless to say, it was, and I've been indebted to Dean Smith ever since."

★ ★ ★

Bill Stern

Nobody Bigger

During the 1930s through the 1950s, there was nobody bigger in sports broadcasting than Bill Stern. He was the voice of sports in America, and he wrote books and newspaper columns, always with a touch of exaggeration. He was much beloved and had a huge following.

From 1965 to 1968, I was the general manager of the Spartanburg Phillies, and we were beginning to attract national attention with our team and promotions. One day, someone said to me, "Did you hear that Bill Stern did his whole national show on you and the Spartanburg Phillies?"

That was the first I had heard of it. I later learned that Stern had read an article in a national trade journal about my work in Spartanburg, and he had proceeded to turn that into his editorial of the night. I was thrilled.

I was twenty-six years old at the time and a huge fan of Stern. I phoned him and thanked him for the national attention he had given me. He said, "Listen, if you're ever in New York, be sure you come by to see me."

Just before Christmas, I was in New York, and I made an appointment to visit with Stern in his office. He surprised me by doing a taped interview with me for another show. He couldn't have been more gracious. To have a big-time sportscasting legend show me such kindness was a huge boost to my confidence and self-esteem.

★ ★ ★

Larry Bird

A Game of H-O-R-S-E

When I moved to Orlando, Larry Bird was coming to the end of his career with the Celtics. On the Celtics' first trip to play the Magic during the 1989–90 season, I requested that Bird come on my radio show, which I broadcast from an Orlando restaurant. Bird joined me on the show for a half hour. It was lunch time, the restaurant was packed, and the patrons were thrilled to see Bird there and to hear him talk about his career.

That night, my twelve-year-old son Bobby was serving as a ball boy. He was out there early during the warm-ups, retrieving balls for Bird. After a while, Bird said to Bobby, "Want to play a game of H-O-R-S-E?"

Bobby swallowed hard, and his eyes got big. He said, "Sure!"

So Bobby Williams and Larry Bird played a game of H-O-R-S-E. Bobby was thrilled and speechless.

The next morning, on the front page of the *Orlando Sentinel*, there was a color photo of Bobby and Bird engaged in their game of H-O-R-S-E. Bobby has it framed in his home today.

That incident gave me a great perspective on Larry Bird. He was an NBA superstar who never lost the common touch, who never stopped caring about kids and thinking about his influence on them. He went out of his way to befriend and influence the next generation.

★ ★ ★

Jesse Jackson

"I Think I Could Have a Positive Influence"

A few years ago, Orlando hosted the NBA all-star weekend. One of the events at the all-star weekend is the annual legends brunch on Sunday, put on by the Retired Players Association. I was one of several people honored at the brunch. Also attending was civil rights leader Jesse Jackson. I've known Jackson since my days as the general manager of the Chicago Bulls.

During the brunch, Jackson took me aside and said, "What's going on with Dwight Howard? What's the young man thinking about?" At that time, our star center was talking openly about wanting to be traded to another team.

"You tell me, Jesse," I said. "We've done all we can to make him happy here in Orlando. I think it would be a big mistake for him to leave."

"Absolutely," Jackson agreed. "Dwight could own this town. He could have a hotel named after him out on the hotel strip if he would remain loyal to this community. He has no business leaving Orlando. I don't usually give out my phone number, but please give Dwight my number. Have him call me. I think I could have a positive influence on him."

So Jackson gave me his number, and I passed it on to Howard. I know that Howard and Jackson talked, and after that conversation, Howard agreed to play one more season in Orlando. But a year later, Howard left Orlando and played for the Lakers for just one season before moving on to the Houston Rockets.

I think Howard has since learned that what Magic co-owner Rich DeVos once said is true: "When a great player leaves, loyalty and love for him are not automatically transferred to the next city." Howard will never have the satisfaction of playing out his career for one team and will never have his number retired. For whatever reason, Howard chose a different path.

Regardless of the outcome, I'm grateful that Jesse Jackson made the effort to have a positive influence on our young star center.

★ ★ ★

E. H. Nelson and Danny Litwhiler

A Lesson in Integrity

From 1940 to 1951, Danny Litwhiler was an outstanding out-fielder who played for the Boston Braves, the St. Louis Cardinals, the Philadelphia Phillies, and the Cincinnati Reds. He was the first major leaguer to play an error-free season. While playing with Cincinnati, he appeared beside Jackie Robinson in a publicity photo to show the world that the formerly all-white team had welcomed its first African-American player. Litwhiler took a lot of flack from bigoted fans and small-minded players, but he was proud of his friendship with Robinson.

Litwhiler credits his family and one great coach for shaping his character. "One of the outstanding mentors in my life," he told me, "was my coach at Bloomsburg State, Dr. E. H. Nelson. He got me into professional baseball. He actually gave me the money so that I could go to my first professional team, and he insisted that I go.

"The reason he gave me money to play pro ball was that I was already playing semipro ball for eighty dollars a month while living at home. If I took the position with the Tigers farm club in Cherleroi, Pennsylvania, I would be paid only seventy-five dollars a month, out of which I'd have to pay room and board plus transportation. So going pro was a step backward financially.

"Dr. Nelson had faith and confidence in me. He believed I had the character qualities—the work ethic, perseverance, and commitment—to become successful in the major leagues. He believed in me more than I believed in myself, and he invested in me."

From Coach Nelson, Litwhiler learned the importance of being a role model. After his playing career ended, Litwhiler coached and managed in the minors for several years. In 1955, he took a position coaching baseball at Florida State University and became known for developing his players as athletes and men of character.

"As a college coach," he told me, "I stressed academic achievement, good character, and proper dress. At rest stops, I told the team before they left the bus, 'Don't take home anything you haven't paid for.' Years later, I got a letter from a former player, now a teacher and coach. He said, 'Remember when you used to say, "Don't take anything you haven't paid for"? Well, my senior year I went to the bookstore as I had for three years and stole all my books for the semester. I went to my room and looked at the books, and your words came to my mind. So I returned the books to the store and never stole again. Thank you for teaching me a lesson in integrity.'

"Over the years, many of the players I coached came back and told me how much I had helped them get a good start in life—not only as baseball players but as men. It brought tears to my eyes to hear them thank me for playing a part in their training and character growth. I could never repay my coach Dr. Nelson. But I think he'd be pleased to know how I repaid his influence in my life by influencing other young men."

★ ★ ★

Bill Veeck

My Mentor

I had the privilege of being mentored by the great baseball owner and innovator Bill Veeck. He presided over some of the storied teams of professional baseball: the Cleveland Indians, the St. Louis Browns, the Chicago White Sox, and the minor league Milwaukee Brewers. As an owner, he never had a door on his office, and he answered his own phone and mail. He was generous in donating his time and advice to me, and he left a lasting imprint on my life. To this day, I try to run my own office as he ran his.

I first met Veeck in 1962 when I was twenty-two years old. Three years later, I completed my first year as the general manager of the Philadelphia Phillies farm club in Spartanburg, South Carolina. It had been a long, tough season because we didn't have a very good team. Despite the team's lackluster performance, however, the fan response was great. We drew 114,000 people to the games. Nevertheless, I was discouraged because our team had finished near the bottom of the rankings.

So I called Veeck. He listened patiently as I poured out all my woes. Then he asked, "Pat, how many people did you draw to the ballpark this season?"

"A hundred fourteen thousand."

"How many of those people had a good time?"

"I think all of them did."

"Tell me one other thing you could have done this summer that would have provided as much fun to that many people."

"I don't think I could have done anything more than I did."

"Pat," he said, "you never have to apologize for showing people a fun time."

During that phone conversation, my outlook was transformed. I realized I was doing something important for thousands of people. While I don't claim to be another Bill Veeck—there will never be another—I've patterned myself after the maestro.

Veeck was my mentor, my role model, and my friend. It was my good fortune to know him and learn from him.

* ★ *

Florence Griffith Joyner and Sugar Ray Robinson

"It Doesn't Matter Where You Come From"

In January 1995, I attended an awards banquet at the Washington Hilton. The highlight of my evening was being seated at the head table next to Florence Griffith Joyner, better known as "Flo-Jo" and "the fastest woman of all time." She was the first American woman to win four medals in one Olympic year—three gold and one silver at Barcelona in 1988—and she set records in the 100- and 200-meter races that still stand today. She passed away in her sleep in 1998 as the result of an epileptic seizure.

During our conversation in 1995, I told Flo-Jo about our daughter Daniela, who was then fourteen and had developed a talent for running. I asked her if she would sign a picture to Dani. "I'd love to," she said, so I gave her our address.

"There's no telling what this might mean in Dani's life," I said.

"Oh, I know!" she said. "Let me tell you my story. I was one of eleven children growing up in South Central Los Angeles. I didn't have much of a future ahead of me. But when I was eight years old, I got to meet Sugar Ray Robinson, the boxing champ."

"What did he say to you?"

"Sugar Ray looked me in the eye and said, 'It doesn't matter where you come from, what your color is, or what the odds are against you. All that matters is that you have a dream, that you believe you can do it, that you commit to doing it.' Right there, I was sold on what my future could be."

A week after I met Flo-Jo in Washington, DC, Dani received a package containing two signed photos and a handwritten letter on Flo-Jo's letterhead. It read:

Dear Dani,

I wish you all the best in athletics and school. If you set a goal, work hard, and believe in yourself, you will accomplish anything you believe in! If you ever have a moment or two, I'd love to hear from you. Take care, Dani, and always follow your dreams!

Love,
Florence Griffith Joyner
Flo-Jo

★ ★ ★

Marian Wright Edelman

"What You Are, Not What You Have"

Marian Wright Edelman grew up under segregation in South Carolina. Her father was a Baptist preacher who taught Marian and her four siblings to serve God and others. He died when Marian was a teenager, and his last words to her were, "Don't let anything get in the way of your education." She studied law at Yale and was the first African-American woman to practice law in Mississippi. She fought hard against poverty, illiteracy, and institutionalized racism. In 1973, she founded the Children's Defense Fund to assist poor children in America. I once interviewed her for a book on character.

"I learned about character," she said, "from my parents and the other adults in my community. The legacies that parents, teachers, and church left to my generation of black children were priceless: faith reflected in daily service, the discipline of hard work and stick-to-it-ness, and a capacity to struggle in the face of adversity.

"Giving up was not part of the language of my elders. You got up every morning, and you did what you had to do. You got up every time you fell down and tried as many times as needed to get it done right. My elders had grit. They valued family life and family rituals and tried to be good role models and expose us to examples of character.

"Role models were of two kinds. First, there were those who achieved in the outside world, like Marian Anderson, my namesake—the contralto who broke the color barrier in the music world and received the UN Peace Prize. Second, there were those who didn't have a lot of education or worldly status but who taught us by the special grace of their lives the message of Christ and Gandhi and Dr. King: The kingdom of God is within you—in what you are, not what you have.

"My role models taught me that the world had a lot of problems, that black people had an extra lot of problems, but that we were obligated to struggle and solve those problems. Being poor was no excuse for not achieving. Extra material gifts bring with them the responsibility of sharing with others less fortunate. I learned that service to others is the rent we pay for living. It's the very purpose of life and not something you do in your spare time."

★ ★ ★

Bart Starr

"The Impact We Have"

In 1967, when I was running the Phillies farm club in Spartanburg, South Carolina, the Packers won Super Bowl I. They were on top of the world, and there was nobody bigger in the sports world than Packers quarterback Bart Starr. I was determined to bring Starr to our ballpark for a personal appearance, even though it really stretched our meager promotions budget to pay an honorarium of five hundred dollars.

Starr came that summer and spent two days at our ballpark. He played golf, did media interviews, signed autographs, and threw passes to the fans on the field at our ballpark. He could not have been more gracious, and we got our money's worth and more. To this day, when I see him or talk to him on the phone, Starr mentions that wonderful summer in 1967.

In August 2010, I spoke at a waste management convention near Greensboro, Georgia. My topic was leadership, and I mentioned how important it is to empower and encourage people. Afterward, a man came up to me and said, "My name is Kevin, and I used to live in Birmingham, Alabama, where I worked on the tail end of a garbage truck. One of the homes on our route belonged to Bart Starr. Many times, he'd come out and ask me how I was doing and give me a word of encouragement. He became like a second father to me. I can't thank him enough. I took his motivational insights to heart, and since then, I've been promoted to management. The impact of Bart Starr on my life will never leave me."

I could hear the emotion in Kevin's voice as he told me that story. Starr's influence had clearly touched him deeply. When I related this story to Starr over the phone, he said, "Isn't it interesting the impact we have on people when we don't even know it?"

We truly never know what kind of influence we have on others. That's why we always need to be aware of how we affect other people. We need to make sure that every word we say, even to the guy who hauls our trash, is a word that uplifts and inspires.

Gil McGregor

The Dirty Shoulders Principle

Former NBA forward Gil McGregor was a broadcaster for
the Charlotte and New Orleans Hornets for more than two
decades. He taught me a concept he calls "The Dirty Shoulders
Principle." He said, "You can tell a guy with a serving attitude
by looking at his shoulders. If his shoulders are dirty, he's a
real servant."

Why dirty shoulders? "Servants get their shoulders dirty when
they lift others up and let them stand tall on their shoulders,"
he explained. "A real servant doesn't care who gets the credit.
Servants just want to lift people up."

McGregor was a friend of the late author-poet Maya Angelou, the Reynolds Professor of American Studies at Wake Forest
University. McGregor once told me, "A group in Winston-Salem
attempted to contact Maya Angelou, hoping she would agree
to cook dinner as a fund-raiser for the March of Dimes. When
they were unable to reach her, someone in the group called me
and said, 'I hear you know Dr. Angelou personally. Would you
be able to help us get in touch with her?' So I called her and
asked if she would help the cause. She immediately said yes. I
thanked her, then added, 'I hope you don't feel I'm using our
friendship in order to get you to volunteer.' She laughed and
said, 'Mr. McGregor, if one cannot be used, it only means that
one is useless.'"

★ ★ ★

Gayle King

Making Faces

In March 2014, I was in New York, where I was interviewed for the *CBS Morning Show* by anchors Gayle King, Charlie Rose, and Norah O'Donnell. The subject of our discussion was *The Mission Is Remission*, my account of my ongoing battle with multiple myeloma. That television appearance gave me a good insight into Gayle King, who is a close friend of Oprah Winfrey as well as a savvy and influential media personality in her own right.

King came into the green room before our segment. She had read the entire book and had two handwritten pages of notes. I was impressed! She wanted to go over her notes with me before we went on the air.

Finally, we went out to the set, and they conducted the interview. All three of my hosts asked excellent questions. It was one of the most thorough and well-prepared interviews I've ever had as an author.

Afterward, I went back to the green room. Moments later, King joined me and asked me a number of questions: "How did you think it went? What could we have done better? Did we ask the right questions? Were there any angles we missed?" She was incredibly caring and wanted to make sure she had given the interview her very best effort—both for my sake and for the sake of the audience.

Then King pointed to a machine in the corner of the green room—a camera that takes a sequence of four pictures. She said, "Pat, I want to get my picture taken with you! Come over here!"

Moments before, she had been totally focused on the interview. In an instant, her mood changed and she became light and chipper. "For the first picture," she said, "let's play it straight. Just smile for the camera. But for the other three, let's clown around and have fun!"

So we got in front of the camera and did our "normal" shot. Then we made faces at the camera for the next three. We were like a couple of kids goofing around in the photo booth at the county fair. We both laughed and had a terrific time.

The next day, she emailed me the pictures, and I have those pictures as souvenirs of an absolutely unforgettable experience. I am now a lifelong fan of Gayle King—a media star who is not only a thoroughly prepared professional but also a deeply caring (and fun-loving) human being.

★ ★ ★

Mitch Albom

A Difference-Maker

I once had Mitch Albom on my radio show to talk about his new book *Have a Little Faith*. I said, "Mitch, what drives you to take on so many challenges and projects in addition to broadcasting and writing?"

"I want to be a difference-maker," he said. "I've been very blessed with the success I've had and the money I've made. Now I have two great passions. One is the problem of homelessness.

I'm deeply immersed in making a difference for the homeless here in Detroit. That's heavy on my heart.

"Second, I feel a burden for the orphans of Haiti. I go down there at least once a month so I can be hands-on in trying to make a difference. I work directly with a number of different orphanages in Haiti. I wish I could tell you thousands of success stories, but it may be just dozens so far. I feel called to that work and to doing what I can to make a difference in as many lives as possible."

★ ★ ★

Eddie Sawyer

"Thanks a Lot, Gene"

You never know how much a simple word of praise or thanks can mean to a player or employee. I learned this profound insight from Gene Conley, who spent eleven seasons in the 1950s and 1960s pitching for the Phillies, Braves, and Red Sox. I once had lunch with Conley, and we talked a lot about baseball. "Gene," I said, "of all the managers and coaches you played for, who do you remember best?"

"Eddie Sawyer," he said instantly. Sawyer managed the Phillies in 1948–52 and 1958–60.

I asked, "What made Eddie Sawyer so memorable?"

"His kindness. Eddie was the kindest manager I ever pitched for."

"Do you have a favorite Eddie Sawyer story?"

"Sure—but I always get emotional when I tell it."

"I'd love to hear it, Gene."

"Back in 1959," he said, "the Phillies were playing a double-header with the Cardinals. It was the bottom of the ninth, and I was in the bullpen. The Cardinals had two on and two out with Stan Musial coming up to bat. Eddie went out to the mound and removed the pitcher, and he waved me out to the mound to pitch." His voice quavered as he remembered.

"What happened?" I asked.

"I struck out Stan Musial," Conley said. "We won. I walked off the field, and Eddie was in the dugout. He shook my hand and said, 'Thanks a lot, Gene. I appreciate that.'" Conley picked up a napkin and dabbed at his eyes.

I waited for the rest of the story—but there wasn't any more. That was it! Why did Conley get so choked up? Because Sawyer said thank you.

There is a profound lesson in that story. Eddie Sawyer probably forgot all about his word of thanks to Gene Conley, but Conley still got emotional over that thank-you decades later.

It doesn't take much to impact others and lift them up.

Part 5

★ ★ ★

Becoming a Person of Excellence

⋆ ★ ⋆

Henry Aaron

The Crack of His Bat

I'll never forget where I was the evening of April 8, 1974. I was in the stands at Atlanta–Fulton County Stadium, along with 53,774 other cheering fans. It was the night of the Atlanta Braves' home opener against the Dodgers, and Henry Aaron was chasing Babe Ruth's career home run record, which had stood for almost four decades.

Dodgers pitcher Al Downing walked Aaron on his first at bat. Aaron's next chance came in the fourth inning. Downing put his first pitch too low, into the dirt. His second delivery was right down the middle—right in Aaron's sweet spot. Aaron took his first swing of the evening. I can still hear the crack of the bat.

The ball sailed in a high arc as Aaron took off running. The ball cleared the glove of Dodgers outfielder Bill Buckner—then cleared the left center field fence. The crowd exploded in cheers as fireworks exploded overhead. A couple of overeager fans clambered over the wall and ran along with Aaron, cheering him on. His teammates poured out of the dugout and surrounded him, whooping and backslapping. Even Aaron's mother ran out onto the field and hugged him.

To this day, few people realize the obstacles Aaron faced on his way to breaking Ruth's record. Those were racially turbulent times, and bigoted fans resented an African-American trying to break Babe Ruth's record. Aaron received more than a hundred thousand hate letters and death threats, but he refused to be deterred.

It took a man of courage to break Babe Ruth's home run record—and Henry Aaron was the man.

★ ★ ★

Ernie Accorsi

Earthy Advice

My friend Ernie Accorsi was the general manager of the NFL's New York Giants for a decade. Before that, he served as the general manager for the Cleveland Browns and the Baltimore Colts. He told me about his first day as a general manager in the National Football League, April 1, 1970.

He had just arrived in the Colts' office when the player personnel director Upton Bell walked up to him and introduced himself. Bell looked rumpled and hurried, and his words were brief: "Welcome to the Colts. Nobody in this league has any guts." Actually, he used a different anatomical reference, but "guts" is close enough. "If you have guts," Bell added, "you will excel in this league." Then he hurried out of the room.

Accorsi never forgot Bell's earthy advice. During his years in

192

the NFL, Accorsi always demonstrated courage—the courage to take risks and to take responsibility for unpopular decisions.

A prime example was Accorsi's 2004 move to acquire Eli Manning as the Giants' quarterback. Manning was the most coveted player in the 2004 NFL draft, but the San Diego Chargers had the first pick. So Accorsi worked out a deal with San Diego. The Chargers would draft Manning, the Giants would then draft Philip Rivers from North Carolina State and would send Rivers plus three draft picks to the Chargers in trade for Manning. It was an audacious trade—and a controversial one. Sportswriters and fans said Accorsi was out of his mind, that he had given away the store—and during Manning's first three seasons with the Giants, the critics appeared to have a point.

Toni Monkovic of the *New York Times* observed that when Accorsi retired at the end of the 2006 season, he was "in danger of being known as the man who threw his legacy away" by giving too much to San Diego in exchange for a rookie QB who didn't pan out.[5] But the very next season, 2007, Manning led the Giants to victory in Super Bowl XLII—and another victory in XLVI to cap the 2012 season.

As Monkovic concluded, Manning "fulfilled the destiny that Accorsi had laid out before him . . . [when he] made his big, bold, gutsy draft-day deal that set this incredible chain of events in motion: the trade that finally landed him his championship quarterback and brought Eli Manning to New York."[6]

Accorsi had guts, and as Bell had predicted, Accorsi excelled in the NFL.

★ ★ ★

Richard B. Myers

Say What You Mean, Mean What You Say

I interviewed General Richard B. Myers about his approach to leadership, and he said, "I grew up in America's heartland, in Kansas. My teachers and coaches were part of the 'greatest generation.' Many of them served in World War II and Korea. They were not boastful about their service; they were simply men and women of quiet integrity. By their actions and through their words, they taught me that integrity means being true to one's values and principles. It means saying what we mean and meaning what we say. It means holding fast to our honor so that we are trustworthy and incorruptible. To be a leader and a role model, you must be a person of integrity, a person who does what is right.

"I remember working for my dad in his business for six months while I was waiting to go into the Air Force. I think those six months shaped me more than any other one experience in my life. My dad taught me how to deal with customers, superiors, and subordinates. He made honesty and integrity the foundational principles of his business practices. He asked me this simple question: 'Are you going to be honest, shade it a little, or be dishonest?' Whenever I face a moral decision, I remember that question."

★ ★ ★

Bill Denehy

Total Honesty

Bill Denehy was a Major League Baseball pitcher in the late 1960s and early 1970s. He once shared with me how he learned the value of living a life of moral principle, character, and honesty.

"I didn't spend much of my early and middle years thinking about character issues," he said. "But on June 15, 1992, I checked into a clinic for drug and alcohol abuse. In rehab, my recovery group taught me about my need to build character. Recovery programs like Alcoholics Anonymous expose your flaws and show you the changes you need to make. Addiction makes people selfish, and I was no exception.

"Not long before I went into rehab, our family was on vacation in Connecticut. My daughter Heather asked me if we could play catch, but being the selfish addict I was, I put it off. We never played catch during that vacation. The day before I went into rehab, I was at one of Heather's softball games, and I said to her, 'Is there something we haven't done that you'd really like to do?' She looked at me with sad eyes and said, 'Let's play catch sometime, Dad.' You'd think that a former pro ballplayer could at least play catch with his daughter, but I had never done it.

"In November 1992, I was out of rehab, and Heather and I finally played catch. We had a great time, and I finally discovered what I'd been missing because of my selfishness.

"You can't overcome addiction without total honesty. You can't lie to yourself and pretend everything is all right when it isn't. You have to address your destructive behavior, your wrong attitudes, your character flaws. Going into recovery opened my eyes to the defects in my character.

"I had sponsors who took me through the Twelve Steps of Alcoholics Anonymous. The fourth step required me to take a 'searching and fearless moral inventory' of myself. A lot of my character defects came out at this point, and I had to address them. My sponsors helped me to overcome the anger and blaming I had developed growing up.

"The twelfth step is that you become a sponsor and a mentor, and you carry the message you've received to other alcoholics who need direction and help. Since I went into recovery, I've sponsored dozens of people. I keep my sobriety by giving it away."

★ ★ ★

George W. Bush

"Tim, You're Forgiven"

I once had former Bush White House official Timothy Goeglein on my radio show to talk about his book *The Man in the Middle*. Goeglein had spent nearly eight years in the Bush White House as a deputy to Karl Rove. I asked him to describe George W. Bush for me.

"He's a man of deep integrity," Goeglein replied. "He says what he means and means what he says. George W. Bush is a rare politician. He's the same in private as he is in public.

"While working in the White House, I wrote a column for

my hometown newspaper. It wasn't a political column. It was about all the other things I love and enjoy in life. And I have to confess that I began plagiarizing those columns.

"One morning, I came back from breakfast and turned on my computer, and there in front of me was an email from a reporter asking if I had plagiarized a recent column in my hometown newspaper. I fell to my knees and said, 'God, help me.' I knew that my life as I had known it was over. I wrote back and told the reporter that it was true.

"I had embarrassed the president. I had embarrassed my colleagues. I had embarrassed my wife and children and all the people who had invested so much in me. I confessed it, and I resigned that afternoon.

"In the political world, when you embarrass the president, there's a kind of divorce that takes place. You get cut off, shunned. I expected that, only that's not what happened to me. Instead, the president's chief of staff, Josh Bolten, told me that 'the boss'—President Bush—wanted to see me. I went to the Oval Office, expecting my woodshed moment. I entered the Oval Office, closed the door, and turned to the president. I said, 'Mr. President, I owe you—' and I was about to make my apology. But he wouldn't even let me apologize. Before I could get the words out, he said, 'Tim, I forgive you.'

"I said, 'But Mr. President, I owe you—' He interrupted me again and said, 'Tim, I've known grace and mercy in my own life, and I am offering it to you now. You are forgiven.'

"I said, 'But Mr. President, you should have taken me by the lapels and tossed me into Pennsylvania Avenue. I've embarrassed you—and after all you have given to me and my family.'

"'Tim, you're forgiven,' he said again. 'Now, we can spend the next few minutes together talking about all this, or we can spend the next few minutes here talking about the last eight years.'

"Then President Bush did something extraordinary. He asked me to sit in the chair of honor below the portrait of George Washington, in front of the fireplace, the place where dignitaries sit. And we had a good talk. Then we prayed together, and we embraced. And I thought, 'This is the last I will ever see of George W. Bush.' Only it wasn't.

"As I was leaving, President Bush asked me to bring my wife and sons to the Oval Office so he could tell them what a great father and husband I am. And sure enough, a few days later, my wife and sons came with me to the Oval Office. The president embraced them, gave them gifts, and we had a wonderful time together. And we've been invited back to the White House a few more times. George W. Bush extended to me the greatest mercy and forgiveness I ever could have experienced, and I am everlastingly grateful."

★ ★ ★

Louis Armstrong

Radiant

In 1955, I was fifteen, my sister Ruthie was twelve, and my dad was an organizer of a fund-raising concert in Wilmington featuring the great Louis Armstrong. Summertime in Delaware can be as hot as blue blazes, and there was no air-conditioning in those days.

Ruthie and I went to the concert, and Armstrong performed

all his great hits: "St. Louis Blues," "All of Me," "Heebie Jee-bies," "Mack the Knife," and more. He puffed out his cheeks when he blew his horn and popped his eyes wide when he sang in that gravel-road voice. He was energetic and joyous, and the sweat poured down his face as he performed.

After the show, my dad said, "Kids, would you like to meet Mr. Armstrong?"

Ruthie and I said, "Sure!"

So we went down to his dressing room. Dad knocked on the door, and Armstrong invited us to enter. I'll never forget that sight. There was Armstrong himself wearing nothing but his boxer shorts, completely drenched in perspiration, a fan blowing air across him as he slathered a greasy salve on his lips. Though he was hot, perspiring profusely, and physically spent, his eyes and smile were radiant. He was happy to greet his young fans.

We chatted with him for a few minutes, and I got to see, at an early age, what it looks like when a performer works hard and gives everything he's got.

★ ☆ ★

Bob Johnson

Needed: Hardworking Young Leaders

Bob Johnson, founder and CEO of Black Entertainment Television (BET), once told me, "I look for young people who are not afraid of hard work. I want them to get in the trenches with me and not just be nine-to-fivers. I want young people who will look at their job as a mission. Call them 'go-to guys,' because no matter what the assignment, they'll get it done. Give me three hardworking young leaders, and I will change the world."

★ ★ ★

Andy Seminick

A Work Ethic That Wouldn't Quit

Andy Seminick spent most of his career with the Philadelphia Phillies as a player, scout, coach, and manager. I first met him when I was a young Phillies fan hanging around Shibe Park. I played for Seminick during my minor league career with the Miami Marlins, and he managed or coached ninety players who got to the major leagues, including Ferguson Jenkins, Mike Schmidt, and John Vukovich.

I became acquainted with John Vukovich in 1967 when I was the general manager of the Spartanburg Phillies. A few years ago, Vukovich shared a story with me about playing for Seminick in the Pacific Coast League.

"Andy Seminick was old-school," he told me. "He had a cast-iron work ethic, and he expected everyone to keep up with him. When I played for him in the Pacific Coast League, we'd play a game in Hawaii, then take an all-night flight back to Portland, Oregon, then take a bus to Eugene. Everybody on the team was lagged out because of the travel and the three-hour time difference. But we didn't go home. We went straight to the ballpark—Andy's orders. We put in a full day of batting practice and infield.

"Andy was older than the rest of us, and you'd think he'd want to get some sleep. Nope. He didn't need sleep, and he figured the rest of us didn't either. And nobody complained. We all knew that Andy had caught in the 1950 World Series with a broken ankle. So no one dared to tell that guy, 'I'm tired.'"

Andy Seminick had a work ethic that just wouldn't quit, and he exemplified that work ethic to his players.

★ ★ ★

Billy Graham

A Big Heart for People

It was 1962, and Billy Graham was at the height of his fame as an evangelist. I was a senior at Wake Forest, and Graham was on campus for two days. So I took my Wollensak tape recorder and went to see him. We had a fascinating conversation. Graham was a big sports fan and had always wanted to be a baseball player. He talked about his baseball background and all the sports he loved to play in his youth and the many athletes he had known. It was one of my best interviews ever.

Graham was on the Wake Forest campus just as our basketball team was heading for the Final Four, so basketball fever was high. We were going up against Ohio State University, headlined by

John Havlicek and Jerry Lucas, in the first game of the Final Four. Graham spent time with Coach Bones McKinney and saw the team bus off as it left to take our players to the airport. As the team boarded the bus, Bones said to Graham, "Billy, I hope you'll be praying for us."

"I will, Bones," Graham said, "but you'd better play good defense on Lucas and Havlicek."

Ten years after my first encounter with Graham, I was the general manager of the Chicago Bulls, and I had become a Christian, so I finally understood Graham's message. He was coming to Chicago for an evangelistic crusade. At his invitation, I went to the McCormick Center and shared my faith before an audience of more than forty thousand people. I later spoke at another Graham crusade in Syracuse, New York.

Every time I was in Graham's presence, I was impressed by two seemingly contradictory facts. First, he has an imposing presence. He's a tall man with striking features, piercing eyes, and an aura of personal magnetism. Whenever Graham enters the room, conversations stop and people take notice. Second, he is a gentle, self-effacing, humble man. If he were not as humble as he is, the personal magnetism of the man would be overwhelming, perhaps even dangerous.

The people who know Graham best all seem to have the same impression of him. He is a figure of greatness wrapped in an almost luminous humility. I once had his youngest daughter, Ruth, on my radio show in Orlando. As we talked, I asked her about her illustrious father. In her rich North Carolina accent, she said, "My daddy knows who he is, a flawed human being. In Daddy's mind, he's still just a farm boy from Charlotte, North Carolina."

I once attended a leadership training session at the Billy Graham Training Center in Asheville, North Carolina. I chatted with

Graham's longtime music director, Cliff Barrows. He described Graham as "a servant-leader with an enlarged heart—a big heart for people. With Billy it's never about power and prestige. It's always about others."

★ ★ ★

Vin Scully

A Matter of Perspective

While conducting research for a book on Coach Vince Lombardi in early 2014, I had the privilege of interviewing eighty-six-year-old Vin Scully, the legendary play-by-play announcer for the Dodgers. Just a few days before I spoke with him, he was honored as the grand marshal of the Rose Parade on New Year's Day in Pasadena. It had been a thrilling day for Scully and his entire family, including his children and grandchildren.

"But I want to put it all in perspective, Pat," he said. "Twenty-four hours after I rode down Colorado Boulevard as grand marshal of the Rose Parade, I was pushing a cart down the aisle at Ralph's Supermarket."

★ ★ ★

Victor Oladipo

Player of the Year and Servant of All

Our phenomenal rookie shooting guard Victor Oladipo was named the *Sporting News* men's college basketball player of 2013 and was the second pick overall in the 2013 NBA draft. When we played the Knicks two days before Christmas 2013, Oladipo played in the first half but sat out the second half.

What did Oladipo do when he wasn't playing? He served as a kind of self-appointed assistant trainer, distributing water during the time-outs. He was, as he put it, "helping to keep the guys hydrated."

Watching Oladipo serving his teammates, I thought, *Wow! Here's the number two draft pick in the entire league, and he's serving his teammates as a water boy. That's a guy who has true humility—and true greatness.*

★ ★ ★

Michael Jordan

Respect

In 1996, the Magic played the Bulls in the Eastern Conference finals of the NBA play-offs—and were dispatched in four games.

It was the year Michael Jordan returned from his foray into baseball, and he was focused and unstoppable. Before game three in Orlando, I was outside the visitors' locker room chatting with the Bulls' team physician, Dr. John Heffernon. I asked him, "Twenty years from now, what will you remember most about Michael Jordan?"

"Aside from the fact that he's the most competitive human being ever to walk the earth and has no fear of failure," he replied, "what I'll remember most is that he respected everybody the same. It doesn't matter if you are the president or the ball boy, the pope or the equipment manager. He treats everyone with respect."

★ ★ ★

Brooks Robinson

"Nothing Worse than a Swelled Head"

Third baseman Brooks Robinson played his entire twenty-three-season career with the Baltimore Orioles. He hit 268 career home runs and earned the league MVP Award (1964) and the World Series MVP Award (1970).

He once told me, "In my first big league game, I went two for four and knocked in a big run. I was eighteen years old. After that game, I ran back to the hotel to call my dad. I was thinking, *Man! I should have been in the majors all along!* Well, on my next eighteen times at bat, I went oh for eighteen, including ten strikeouts. Being humbled like that was the best thing that could happen to me. There's nothing worse than a ballplayer with a swelled head. That dose of humility gave me a more realistic perspective, and it made me a better baseball player and a better person."

★ ★ ★

Alvin Dark

A Lesson in Humility

Alvin Dark, a longtime major league shortstop and manager, told me about a lesson he learned during the 1949 season. "I was with the Boston Braves," he said, "and we were playing in Pittsburgh at Old Forbes Field. Johnny Cooney was the manager of the team, and late in the game he took me out for a pinch hitter. I went absolutely berserk! I took my bat and went into a little room behind the dugout. There was a wooden wheelbarrow in that room, and I started smashing that wheelbarrow to bits with my bat. It sounded like a rifle shot every time I hit that thing. I was totally out of control.

"After the game, I sat on a stool in front of my locker. My teammate Eddie Stanky sidled over to me and said very quietly, 'So you're Babe Ruth, huh? Not allowed to pinch-hit for you, huh?' I could have pinched Stanky's head off, but he was right. I learned a great lesson in humility that day."

★ ★ ★

Marvin Lewis

Talent versus Character

Marvin Lewis is the head coach of the Cincinnati Bengals. He once told me about a hard lesson he learned as a coach at the university level. During the recruiting season, Lewis heard about a talented junior college linebacker who was being courted by several universities. He asked his assistants and scouts why they had not suggested recruiting this player. To a man, they all agreed that this young player was a bad apple. He was loaded with talent, but he was arrogant and uncoachable. "Steer clear of him," they said.

"But I didn't listen," Lewis admitted to me. "I recruited the guy based on talent alone. Turned out he was nothing but trouble. Even worse, his bad character and bad attitude infected two other promising players, including a talented freshman. What a rough year that was! I learned my lesson. Talent is important, but character is essential."

★ ★ ★

Martin Luther King Jr.

The Content of His Character

My Minor League Baseball career came to an end in the summer of 1963. So I packed my belongings and prepared to trek from Miami to Bloomington, Indiana. My goal was to complete a master's degree in physical education at Indiana University. I called my mother and told her my plans. "Mom," I said, "I'm going to visit you in Wilmington before I head to Indiana."

"Pat," she said, "instead of you coming to Wilmington, why don't we meet in Washington, DC? Carol and I are going to the March on Washington to hear Martin Luther King Jr. He's giving a speech at the Lincoln Memorial on August 28."

I wasn't surprised. Mom was a lifelong Democrat and had been active in social causes for as long as I could remember. She had spoken glowingly of King ever since the 1955 Montgomery bus boycott. I agreed to meet Mom and my sister Carol in DC. I'll always be grateful to Mom because—thanks to her—I became a witness to history.

Mom, Carol, and I were in the vast crowd before the Lincoln Memorial on that hot, humid day. I saw actors Sidney Poitier, Marlon Brando, and Charlton Heston give stirring speeches about justice. Mahalia Jackson sang "How I Got Over," Bob Dylan sang "Only a Pawn in Their Game," and Peter, Paul, and Mary performed Dylan's "Blowin' in the Wind."

But the main event was King. We stood about fifty yards away from him off to one side but close enough to make out his expression as he spoke. I didn't grasp the historic importance of his speech at the time, yet my emotions were stirred as King's words wafted over the crowd like a cooling breeze. It was not a long speech, just a little over seventeen minutes. Yet his words set our nation on a new course of freedom and justice.

Near the end of the speech, Mahalia Jackson shouted, "Tell them about the dream, Martin!"

And I heard King say, "I have a dream that one day this nation will rise up and live out the true meaning of its creed: 'We hold these truths to be self-evident, that all men are created equal.' . . . I have a dream that my four little children will one day live in a nation where they will not be judged by the color of their skin but by the content of their character."

Less than five years after he spoke those words, King was felled by an assassin's bullet, but the dream I heard about that day still lives.

★ ★ ★

Watson Spoelstra

On the Celestial Curbstone

Watson "Waddy" Spoelstra was a sportswriter for the *Detroit News* from 1945 to 1973. He covered the Detroit Lions and Tigers for years, and he described himself as a "hard-drinking hell-raiser."

In 1957, Spoelstra's eighteen-year-old daughter suffered a life-threatening brain hemorrhage. He went to his knees and offered his life to God if he would spare her life. Spoelstra's daughter recovered, and he kept his promise and committed his life to Christ. He was mentored in his faith by Detroit Lions defensive end Bill Glass.

During his sportswriting days, Spoelstra noticed that many baseball players were unable to attend church because of the game schedules. When he retired from sportswriting in 1973, he founded an organization called Baseball Chapel, which provided pregame chapel services to the players. He got a great lift when baseball commissioner Bowie Kuhn not only okayed the chapels but also gave Spoelstra ten thousand dollars to get the organization started.

I served on Spoelstra's board for a while, and he was like a kind old grandfather. He'd say to me, "I'm going to get to heaven first. I'll be on the celestial curbstone waiting for you." Since Spoelstra's death in 1999, I've often thought of him in heaven waiting for me on that celestial curbstone.

★ ★ ★

James Dobson

No Fear of Death, But . . .

I first met James Dobson during an interview about a book I had cowritten. I appeared on his radio show a number of times and have built a nice friendship with him. Dobson is a great sports fan, and he loves to talk basketball and play basketball.

One year, I had the responsibility of coordinating the chapel service for the all-star weekend in Denver. I invited Dobson to be our speaker at the event, and he accepted. I sat with him at one of the ballgames the Saturday night before he spoke. We had a couple of hours to talk about sports, life, and spiritual matters.

At one point, I asked him if he feared death.

"No, I don't fear death itself," he said, "but I do fear all you have to go through before you die. I fear poor health, suffering, old age, illness, the loss of vigor. I'm not looking forward to that part of life, but I have no fear of death itself."

★ ★ ★

Stu Inman

"I'm Ready"

In 1969, Stu Inman helped build the Portland Trail Blazers expansion franchise. He drafted the legendary Bill Walton and was the architect of the Trail Blazers' 1976–77 NBA championship team (the team that knocked our Philadelphia 76ers out of the NBA finals). Inman was my friend for almost forty years.

In early 2007, I picked up the newspaper and read that Inman had died of a heart attack at age eighty. He had passed away in his Lake Oswego, Oregon, home. I called his widow, Eleanor, and she told me, "Stu was in his closet, getting dressed to start the day, when he simply collapsed. I rushed to his side where he lay on the floor, and his last words were, 'Lord, I'm ready.' He was gone before the paramedics could get there."

Inman was a man of faith, and his faith carried him safely into eternity with his Lord.

★ ★ ★

John Wooden

Coach

In July 2000, I checked my voice mail and heard a message that changed my life. "Mr. Williams," the caller said, "this is John Wooden, former basketball coach at UCLA." Coach Wooden went on to give his personal recommendation for a UCLA trainer who had applied for a position with the Magic. Then he added, "I enjoy reading your books very much. Good-bye."

I returned his call, and we had a wonderful chat. It was the first of many happy encounters I would have with Coach John Wooden. Months later, when I asked his blessing on a book to be called *How to Be like Coach Wooden*, he left another voice mail, saying, "Mr. Williams, this is John Wooden, former basketball coach at UCLA. I received your letter and though I'm not worthy of a project like this, if you would like to write this book, you go right ahead." Wooden was a one-of-a-kind human being, a sports legend who seemed completely unaware of his fame or, at least, completely unfazed by it.

Our friendship grew, and I produced more books about

Wooden's life and philosophy. During the last decade of his life, I had many inspiring visits and conversations with him. I also interviewed hundreds of people who knew him.

On several occasions, I went to Wooden's condo in Encino, California, to pick him up. At five o'clock sharp, we'd head out to the Valley Inn in Sherman Oaks—Wooden's favorite dining spot. As we chatted over dinner, I was amazed by the depth of his wisdom and the quickness of his gentle sense of humor.

Then we'd return to his condo, and he'd recite his latest poem while the Mills Brothers harmonized on his old-fashioned phonograph. Wooden didn't like digitized music—nothing but velvety smooth vinyl for him.

If the light on his answering machine was blinking, he'd check the machine to see who had called. He often received calls from former players. Some called to ask advice. Others just called to say hello. His players clearly loved him. And why not? He certainly loved them.

Wooden's beloved wife, Nell, died on March 21, 1985. After her death, he began a tradition of writing a love letter to Nell on the twenty-first day of each month. He told her that he loved her and looked forward to seeing her again. He sealed each letter in an envelope and set it on the pillow on Nell's side of the bed. Once, when I was at his condo, Wooden showed me his bedroom, and that little bundle of love letters was right there, tied with a yellow ribbon.

On Friday, June 4, 2010, Wooden went to be with the Lord—and with Nell. A number of Wooden's players visited him in the hours before he passed away. One was Jamaal Wilkes, who went to see Wooden the day before he died. Wilkes later reported that Wooden got out of bed and shaved, saying, "I'm getting ready to go see Nellie."

It was an incredible privilege for me to get to know Wooden

during the final decade of his life. I got to see him take his victory lap, and he left a deep imprint on my life. Though I was never one of his players, I often found myself wanting to please him, wanting to make him proud of me.

In fact, I still do.

* * *

Wendell Kempton

Lots of Balloons

Wendell Kempton was a Christian leader, a Bible teacher, and a friend to many leading sports figures. He was a chapel speaker at three Super Bowls and a World Series. The list of athletes, coaches, and sports executives he mentored includes Joe Gibbs, Mike Schmidt, Julius Erving, Bobby Jones, and Pat Williams. I got to know him when I was the general manager of the 76ers. His teaching was a source of strength for many of our players.

Once, I talked to him about death and eternity. "Wendell," I said, "I don't want to die. I know as a Christian I shouldn't feel that way, but I can't help it. I look forward to heaven, but I have no interest whatsoever in dying."

"Pat," he said, "that's perfectly normal. But you need to understand that there are three kinds of grace God gives to us in this life. First, he gives us saving grace when we commit our lives to him. Second, he gives us living grace—the drive, focus, and energy for living each day so that we can do our work with zeal and enthusiasm. Third, he gives us dying grace. When the time comes for you to leave this world, God will prepare you for it, and the transition will be easy."

That conversation gave me comfort.

In late 2007, at age seventy-five, Kempton began to make the transition from living grace to dying grace. He noticed a growth on his arm and began experiencing flu-like symptoms. He went to the hospital, where tests revealed that his body was riddled with a previously undetected cancer. He had only weeks to live. It was time for him to say good-bye to his wife, Ruth, and their six children and twenty grandchildren.

It was a blessing that Kempton had the time and the strength to plan his own funeral. While he was dictating his funeral plans to his son Tim, his six-year-old granddaughter Audrey tiptoed into the room.

"What are you doing, Pop-Pop?" Audrey asked.

"I'm planning a party," Kempton said.

"Will there be balloons?"

"Yes, indeed!"

Kempton had one of his associates call me. "Pat Williams knows all the sports people in my life," he said, "and Pat will make sure they all come to the funeral." When I got the word, I asked six of Kempton's friends from the sports world to speak.

By Saturday, January 5, it was clear that Kempton's fight was nearly over. His oldest son, Stan, stayed with him through the night. Before sunrise on Sunday morning, Stan remembered that one of his dad's favorite Sunday morning greetings was, "Good morning, it's resurrection day!" So Stan leaned close to his dad's ear and said, "Dad, it's resurrection day. It's Sunday morning, your favorite day of the week. You've done your job, and you're going to your eternal reward. Get your best sermon ready, Dad. You're going into glory." With those words, Stan ushered his dad from this life into eternal life.

Kempton's funeral was held on January 11, 2008. I introduced the six men who had come to talk about his influence on their lives: Bobby Jones, Mike Schmidt, Bob Boone, Garry Maddox, Terry Harmon, and Doug Collins. They shared how Kempton had introduced them to the Lord or helped them grow in the Lord.

It was clear to me that God gave Kempton all three kinds of grace. His "going-home party" was a great celebration of a life well lived and triumphantly completed.

And just as Kempton promised, there were lots of balloons.

Notes

John F. Kennedy

1. Richard Schickel, *Intimate Strangers: The Culture of Celebrity* (New York: Fromm, 1986), 233.

Larry Catuzzi

2. After his daughter Lauren was killed aboard United Flight 93, which crashed in Pennsylvania on September 11, 2001, Larry Catuzzi became cochairman of the Flight 93 Memorial Task Force and director of the Flight 93 Federal Advisory Commission.

Robin Roberts

3. Jay Busbee, "Nelson Mandela: 'Sport Has the Power to Change the World,'" Yahoo! Sports, December 5, 2013, http://sports.yahoo.com/blogs/the-turnstile/nelson-mandela-sport-power-change-world-215933270.html.

Tony Dungy

4. Art Stricklin, "Tony Dungy Voices the Pain and Lessons from His Son's Suicide," *Baptist Press*, February 3, 2006, http://www.bpnews.net/printerfriendly.asp?id=22595.

Ernie Accorsi

5. Toni Monkovic, "First Chapter: Eli Manning," *The Fifth Down: The New York Times NFL Blog*, October 29, 2008, http://fifthdown.blogs.nytimes.com/2008/10/29/first-chapter-eli-manning/?_php=true&_type=blogs&_r=0.

6. Ibid.

You can contact Pat Williams at:

Pat Williams
c/o Orlando Magic
8701 Maitland Summit Boulevard
Orlando, FL 32810
phone: 407-916-2404
pwilliams@orlandomagic.com

Visit Pat Williams's website: www.PatWilliams.com
On Twitter: @OrlandoMagicPat

If you would like to set up a speaking engagement with Pat Williams, please call or write his assistant, Andrew Herdliska, at the above address or call 407-916-2401. Requests can also be faxed to 407-916-2986 or emailed to aherdliska@orlandomagic.com.

We would love to hear from you. Please send your comments about this book to Pat Williams at the above address. Thank you.

CONNECT WITH PAT

We would love to hear from you. Please send your comments about this book to Pat Williams:

pwilliams@orlandomagic.com

Pat Williams
c/o Orlando Magic
8701 Maitland Summit Boulevard
Orlando, FL 32810

If you would like to set up a speaking engagement for Pat, please contact his assistant, Andrew Herdliska:
(407) 916-2401
aherdliska@orlandomagic.com

PATWILLIAMS.COM

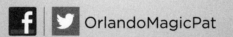 OrlandoMagicPat

WHEN YOU LIVE
as if every day counts ... *it does.*

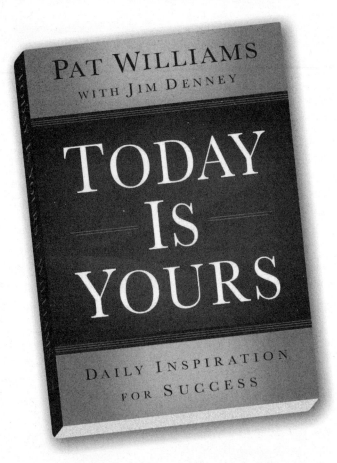

Start each day of the year with an inspiring quote, story, or
anecdote from some of Pat's best-loved books.

Revell
a division of Baker Publishing Group
www.RevellBooks.com

Pat Williams has known the thrill of victory and the agony of defeat—both on the sidelines of the basketball court and in his personal life.

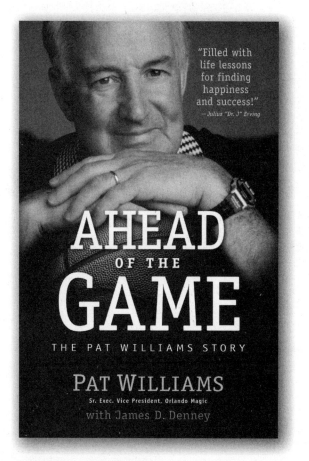

In *Ahead of the Game* he offers you ten principles for success from his own unpredictable life and career that will inspire you to live a winning life despite your challenges.

COACH JOHN WOODEN
One of the Greatest Coaches
of All Time

COACH
WOODEN'S
GREATEST
SECRET

The Power of
a Lot of Little Things
Done Well

Pat Williams
with Jim Denney

The **7** Principles
That Shaped
His Life and Will
Change Yours

*"Coach Wooden didn't
just teach basketball—
he taught life."*
TONY DUNGY

COACH
WOODEN

PAT WILLIAMS
with JIM DENNEY
Foreword by TONY DUNGY

℞ **Revell**
a division of Baker Publishing Group
www.RevellBooks.com